Emil Agayev

BAKU

A Guide

Raduga Publishers
Moscow

Эмиль Агаев

БАКУ

Путеводитель

На английском языке

Редакция литературы по спорту и туризму

Translated from the Russian
Edited by *Amanda Calvert*

Editor of the Russian text *Marta Derzhavina*
Editor of the English text *Irina Vishnevskaya*
Designed by *Alla Popova*
Art Editor *Alexandra Tomchinskaya*
Maps by *Lyubov Cheltsova*
Layout by *Alexandra Agafoshina*
Photos by *Isaac Rubinchik, Viktor Polyakov*

© Издательство "Радуга", 1987г.

English translation © Raduga Publishers 1987

$A \dfrac{1905040100\text{-}308}{031(01)\text{-}87} 063\text{-}87$

ISBN 5-05-001183-3

CONTENTS

Salam! 4
General Information 6

THE CAPITAL OF "THE LAND OF FLAMES". HISTORICAL BACKGROUND

History. Early period 13
Beginnings of Baku 14
"Rock Oil" 15
12th–16th Centuries 16
The Azerbaijan Safevide State 18
Unity with Russia 19
An Oil Capital 20
Path of Progress 23
Revolutionary Struggle 24
The Baku Commune 25
28th of April 26
Socialist Construction 28
Baku Today 30

TOURS ROUND BAKU

Round Tour 39
From the Old City to the Seafront 72
Modern Baku 107
From the City Centre to the Former Suburbs 141

TOURS OUTSIDE BAKU

Kobustan 157
Apsheron 164
Sumgait—Khoudat—Kubá 175
Shemakha—Sheki—Zakataly 183

PRACTICAL INFORMATION 191

Salam!

Salam and **Hosh galmisian** *(Welcome) are the traditional greetings in Baku, one of the largest cities in the Soviet Union and capital of Soviet Azerbaijan, where guests have always been regarded as a blessing. Baku is honoured and happy to receive the numerous visitors who flock to it, attracted by its unique position and varied architecture, its cult of poetry and music and, of course, by its people.*

Visitors to Baku are sure to find good friends who will be delighted to show them round the streets and boulevards, the medieval walled city and the derricks of the oldest-known oil-fields in the world. They will

*be introduced to the classical **mugam** singing popular in Azerbaijan and to the niceties of the local cuisine. They will be taken to see the prehistoric rock-carvings in Kobustan and, by way of contrast, the modern offshore oil platforms, to mention just two out of many other fascinating sights.*

This guide-book is intended to provide information on the history as well as on the present-day life of Baku.

***Salam! Hosh galmisian!** You are welcome to the capital of Soviet Azerbaijan.*

Fresco from the Sheki Khans' Palace.

GENERAL INFORMATION

The map of the Azerbaijan Soviet Socialist Republic is shaped somewhat like an eagle in flight with Baku for its head.

Baku is situated on the Apsheron Peninsula, which juts about 40 miles out into the Caspian Sea, at the point where the slopes of the Great Caucasus Range descend to the sea.

The low shoreline with its historic coastal road is protected here by the mountains. Hills, about 1,150–1,300 ft. high form a natural amphitheatre with a convenient harbour—an ideal location for a city. They also provide good limestone for building. Combine all this with the fabulous local mineral resources of which Jules Verne once wrote that to obtain instant heating and lighting all you need to do is to make a hole in the ground and natural gas will gush out—and it will be understood why from earliest times man decided to settle at this spot.

Millions of years back the land here was under the sea. Later on movements in the earth's crust led to the formation of dry land. The land-locked Caspian is in fact the largest lake in the world, and over the centuries has had seventy (!) different names. The present level of the Caspian, which in the course of its history has advanced on dry land and receded several times, is 90 ft. below that of the World Ocean and it is still constantly changing. At Baku latitude the sea does not freeze over and Baku port is open all the year round.

In many respects, the Caspian, however, deserves its name of "sea": it has a surface area of

400,000 sq.km., salinity (13 lb per 1,00016 of water, as compared to 16 lb of that of the Black Sea), and it is subject to frequent storms (force 8-9).

Baku has a moderately warm and dry subtropical climate, with a hot summer and short mild winter. Frosts occur once in 10-15 years. The average temperature is 3-4 °C above zero in January, 25-26 °C in July. On the same latitude as Greece and Italy, the Apsheron Peninsula is warmer and drier. Incidentally, its average yearly temperature of 14.4 °C coincides with that of the Earth. It has the greatest number (284) of fine days in the year of all places in the Caucasus, and the least amount of rainfall (180 mm in the south, 322 mm in the north).

The prevailing winds are either from the south—*Hilavar*, or the north—*Hazri*, i.e., Caspian. The *Hazri* is in fact a very strong sea wind channelled onto the Apsheron Peninsula by the mountains. These gale force winds which, as a medieval geographer tells us, were known to drive flocks of sheep and herds of horses to the sea, complicate the work of sailors, oilmen and fishermen and make the weather changeable.

There is a story about a traveller who came home with a report that during the four days he had spent in Baku he had witnessed the four seasons of the year. Yet, on the whole, the *Hazri* is a kind of blessing for it blows fresh air through this huge industrial city and moderates the summer heat.

Due to the hot, dry, windy climate there is comparatively little vegetation on the peninsula. The Eldar pine, requiring little moisture, is the species of tree that grows best here. The only river, the Sumgait, dries up in summer. Hence, the necessity for irrigation which has been increasingly developed in recent years.

Baku today is a city of gardens and parks. Each citizen is required to plant a certain number of trees. As a result there is now 20 sq.m. of greenery per head, a ratio higher than in London, Rome or Bucharest.

The first thing a traveller notices upon arrival in Baku is its unique smell: a peculiar mixture of dry mountain air tempered with oil and gas, "wonderful and unforgettable", as visiting Russian writers have more than once described it.

Present-day Baku with suburbs, their complex of oil-wells and refineries, industrial, agricultural zones and holiday belts, extends over the whole peninsula, as well as to the numerous offshore islands, both natural and artificial, where the oilmen live and work. It includes, for example, the steel platform township, known as Oil Rocks, 60 miles out to sea. Greater Baku thus occupies an area of 220,000 hectares (as compared to the 22 hectares of the historical centre of the town).

Administratively Baku is divided into eleven districts in which there live over 1.6 million people, or about half of the republic's total urban population. In terms of population Baku ranks fifth among Soviet towns after Moscow, Leningrad, Kiev and Tashkent, and it occupies fourth place—coming ahead of Tashkent—in economic potential.

The capital of Azerbaijan is one of the most multinational cities in the country. Apart from Azerbaijanis (55.7%) there are representatives of about 80 other nationalities living here including Russians (22%), Armenians (14.1 %), and other Caucasian peoples, as well as Jews, Tatars and Ukrainians.

This great variety of nationalities is explained historically by the population influx during the oil boom at the turn of the century, and another, more organized one, after 1920, when post-war economic rehabilitation made necessary aid from other regions. Today the population influx has dropped and is mostly accounted for by Azerbaijanis.

> An Azerbaijani family is usually close-knit and affectionate. Obedience to the older generation, and hospitality to visitors are traditional. The host will go out of his way to please his guest. The wife is usually a good cook, while it is the man traditionally who goes to market.

The average city family consists of 4–5 persons. Women, who live longer, slightly outnumber the men. With 45 people aged over a hundred per 100,000 of population, Azerbaijan and neighbouring Georgia hold the world record for longevity.

Several factors may account for this: the mountain climate, genes, the rare medicinal herbs, the steady rhythm of life, healthy toil in the fresh air plus a lot of walking over the hills, and a balanced diet. Another contributing factor may be that the old, as a rule, tend to live with their children, grand-children and great grand-children, enjoying their love and respect. They continue to be active long after retirement age.

Baku too has a good record for long livers: in 1985 there were 1,400 persons over 90, and 120 aged over a hundred living in the city. Despite the disadvantages of life in an urban environment, genetic and psychological factors presumably play a role here plus the fact that Baku has become a much cleaner place to live in thanks to a lot of greenery planted in recent years and anti-pollution measures.

In addition to its remarkable longevity rate, Azerbaijan boasts the youngest population in the USSR: due to a high birth rate and low infant mortality over half of its people are under 30. Come and see for yourself: this is a country of active old age and of beautiful children.

The Capital of the "Land of Flames"

Historical Background

History, Early Period

Since the earliest times, this area has been known as "the land of flames". Baku's coat of arms bears three torches on a field of sea waves.

The tribes who inhabited this land in antiquity, the forerunners of the Azerbaijani people, occupied a vast territory which included both Northern (now Soviet) and Southern (Iranian) Azerbaijan. Various parts of it became known after the tribes as Caspian, Mannai, Media, and Caucasian Albania. Some of the states which emerged in the area from the 3rd millennium B. C. were powerful and relatively advanced, particularly Mannai and Media, the latter subjugating Assyria, and Urartu among others.

In the 8th century B. C. the land was raided and settled by the Scythians coming from the Black Sea area and Northern Caucasus. In the 6th century B. C. Media was conquered by the Persians and came to form part of the Persian Empire. The Medes were to have a strong influence on Persian culture.

At the end of the 4th century B. C. the Persian Empire fell prey to the troops of Alexander the Great. King of Minor Media, Atropat, seized this moment to proclaim his country's independence. The lands north of the river Araks were called Atropatena after him. Later the area came to be known by the Persians as Aturpatakan, by the Armenians as Atrapatakan, by the Arabs as Azerbaijan... In time the latter name was extended to include the present territory of the republic, previously known as Caucasian Albania. That the name Azerbaijan survived may probably be due to the fact that it is thought to have had another meaning, viz "a land of flames", which was connected with the cult of fire, practised by the people of ancient Azerbaijan.

The earliest cave man habitation to have been found in the USSR, was discovered here in the Azykh cave. Apart from human jaw-bones and stone tools and implements the cave contained primitive hearths and evidence of fire-worship. The same cult is reflected in numerous later legends, traditions and customs handed down from generation to generation.

Beginnings of Baku

There is nothing legendary, however, about the "flaming rock" to be seen near the village of Mahomedly in the Apsheron steppe. A rocky slope covered with flaming torches of escaping methane, which have been burning, it is thought, almost ever since the time of Alexander the Great, must have appeared like a miracle to the fire-worshippers.

The name of Baku may be also connected with Zoroastrianism if it is derived, as is maintained by the historian and archaeologist, Professor Sara Ashurbeili, a leading expert in the field, from the word "bak"—which in a number of ancient languages means "sun", "god", rather than from the word "wind" or "hill" as other scholars believe. The word, presumably, came to be used both as a name for the tribes or sects of fire-worshippers, *bakans*, who inhabited these parts, and as a name for the city.

The exact age of Baku, undoubtedly a very ancient city, is difficult to determine. Numismatic and archaeological evidence goes back to the 5th century A.D. The first written record we have for the town was made by an Arab geographer in 930 A.D. The earliest excavations in the *Icheri-Shekher* (Old City) revealed a densely populated area with the remains of houses and other buildings, a lot of pottery and other finds dating from the 5th to 8th century. The first reference to the flames near Baku comes in a description of the Scythian route and takes us back to the first centuries A.D. Some historians ascribe the foundation of Baku to Darius (c. 6th century B.C.). The English scholar F. Petrie identified Baku with "the mountain of the rising sun, Vakhau" in the Egyptian *Book of the Dead* (2nd-3rd millennium B.C.), and suggested that its name derived from *baka* meaning "dawn", Baku being situated on the

Eastern slopes of the Caucasus...

However that may be, it is certain that human settlements existed on Apsheron several thousand years prior to the Christian era. A dried-up oil lake has been discovered near Baku which 35–40 thousand years ago attracted animals by its deceptive gleam. Coming here to drink they got stuck and died to be well preserved together with plants and fruit. Abundant flora and fauna attracted human habitation. This is confirmed by the traces of charcoal. Finally, there is Kobustan with its primitive settlements and famous rock-carvings, some of them 10 thousand years old.

Rock Oil

Besides the flames of "god's city", the Mecca of ancient fire-worshippers, oil was another attraction bringing people to Baku: it was used for lighting and heating, to burn lime and even as medicine. It was also utilized in thickened form for roof insulation. "It is not used in cooking, but burned in lamps, and used as a cure for a number of ailments," wrote Marco Polo. Other travellers noted with surprise that "white oil" was taken for "the gallstone disease and tender joints", and "taken orally for weak chests, headaches, venereal disease and stones it brought relief". It was also utilized as ointment "to rub the hides of camels to prevent the formation of scabs". It was used for making varnish and lacquer, for cleaning clothes and removing stains, as paint thinner, etc.

But it was valued most of all in warfare: the "Greek fire" must have contained it, it was used by the Mongols and Arabs as a weapon, the latter had a special detachments of flame-throwers. Up to the spread of fire-arms in the 16th century, oil was widely used in warfare. So the oil-wells of Apsheron were jealously guarded by the medieval fortresses of the local feudal lords. They were also taxed.

Up to the 9th century oil was simply collected on the surface with the help of cloth, transported by caravan and by sea in sealskins obtained from the Caspian. Later wells were sunk and the oil was scooped out in leather bags. A device somewhat like a multi-dipper crane was invented. Shelters, sometimes made of stone, were constructed over the wells to make work possible in any weather. Daily output amounted to 200 camel packs, or about 60 tonnes. Oil was stored in earth reservoirs. Refining techniques became known on Apsheron from the 13th century.

But obviously the demand for "rock" or "mineral" oil at that time was in no way comparable to what it is today. Baku's hour had yet to come. As a port on a little-known inland sea, Baku was also of limited importance. It was only in 1720, under Peter the Great, that the first map of the Caspian was made. The strategic route along the coast, leading to the Derbent Pass, running between the sea and the mountains, was of far greater importance. But, alas, it was not wholly beneficial: bringing trade, wealth and life, it also brought conquest, destruction and death. Nomads from the north, conquerors from the south made use of the route. Patiently suffering repeated sackings and destruction, Baku continued to live its own life, biding its time in anticipation of great things to come. Far from the centre of the vast territory inhabited by the nascent Azerbaijani people, it was not to become the capital for a long time to come, a brilliant succession of other cities gaining prominence before it: ancient Tabriz, Kabbala, Barda, and later Nakhichevan, Ganja, Shemakha.

12th–16th Centuries

The rise to prominence from the beginning of the 11th century of the hitherto obscure Shirvan-Shahs' state brought the region closer to the centre of events. It was in the 12th century that Baku first became a capital. Driven out of Shemakha by a rival state, Shirvan-Shah Ahsitan I moved his residence, if only briefly, to Baku. It was Absitan I who commissioned the famous poem *Layla and Majnun* from the great Nizami.

Baku was fortified and embellished. To protect their strong fleet the Shirvan-Shahs built a fortress in the bay. Later to be submerged under water, this was presumably the semi-legendary Sabayil whose ruins have been recently explored. In one of his *kassydi* (odes), another great Azerbaijan poet, Hagani, mentions Baku's impregnable defences and its significance among oriental cities. In the 12th century a new wall was built round the city and the Maiden Tower finished and included in the system of defences. In the 13th century the city successfully withstood a long seige by the Mongols and only surrendered when the whole country, as well as Georgia and Armenia, had been overrun.

Early in the 15th century the country managed to rid itself of the Mongol yoke. Shirvan and Baku retained their independence for almost a hundred years. The enterprising and wily Ibrahim I was able to appease Tamerlane so that the country was spared a heavy tribute.

> There is a story of Ibrahim going to negotiate with Tamerlane and taking various presents with him—nine of each kind, apart from slaves of which there were only eight. "I am your ninth slave," he said. His son, Halilullah I, carried on the policy of appeasement, avoiding war, and promoting peaceful construction. During his reign Baku was again made capital and a palace was built in the old city, the palace of Shirvan-Shahs, a remarkable piece of architecture which is well preserved to this day.

By the 14th century Baku already had a mint and a fairly advanced economy and trade. Colonies of merchants from Persia, India and Bukhara mushroomed in the city where they lived in caravanserais specially built for them, some of which are still to be seen today. New oil-wells were sunk, oil was exported to all corners of the world via caravans and boats. By the 15th century Baku had become the most important Caspian port overshadowing its rival—Derbent. More Russian ships called at it now that Russia, having finally thrown off the Mongol yoke (1480), was developing its economic and political links.

The Azerbaijan Safevid State

The significant point of difference between the Azerbaijanis and Ottoman Turks was that they belonged to two different branches of the Islamic faith: the Ottoman Turks were Sunnites, while the Azerbaijanis (as the Persians) were predominantly Shiites. Whereas in the Middle Ages Turkey became a centre for Sunnite Islam, Persia became a centre for the Shiite faith.

In 1500 Ismail of the Safevid dynasty seized power by defeating the Shirvan-Shahs with the help of the *gysilbashi* ("redheads", from the red-striped headdress they wore), troops of Shiite fanatics of Azerbaijan origin. Two years later, Ismail, also an Azerbaijani, seized Tabriz and proclaimed himself Shah. Thus the Safevid state with Azerbaijan for its centre was founded and played a significant part in the history of the nation, uniting under its rule all the Azerbaijan lands.

The Azerbaijan language was used not only in everyday speech but also for poetry, science, at court, in the army and for diplomatic correspondence. It was the first time that such a wide breach had been made in the cult of Pharsi and Arabic. National culture flourished under Safevid rule. Ismail Shah himself was an excellent poet known in Azerbaijan literature as Hattai.

Baku, as the Shirvan-Shahs' capital, suffered repeated attacks and was sacked as Ismail put down the resistance of the Shirvan dynasty. The palace of the Shirvan-Shahs was stripped of its gold and silver and fell into decay.

The Safevids set out on a series of conquests overrunning within a short time Persia, Iraq, part of Armenia, of what is now Soviet Central Asia, Anatolia and Afghanistan.

They clashed with Turkey—a great battle being fought near Tabriz between the Sultan's 200,000-strong army and Ismail's "redheads". Intermittent warfare was to continue between the Safevids and Ottoman Turkey for about a hundred years.

Despite the Turkish expansion Russian and European merchants stepped up their trade with Persia and India via the Caspian and Baku, which grew steadily as a result. The city's importance, nevertheless, appeared to be on the wane.

Unity with Russia

Under Shah Abbas I Persian influence became predominant in the Safevid state with Azerbaijan being reduced to the status of a mere province: he curbed the power of the Azerbaijan warrior nobles and raised that of the Persian clergy and officials, moved the capital from Tabriz to Isfaghan, and made Pharsi the state language. Now Azerbaijan had to fight both Ottoman Turkey and Persia.

The situation was made worse by Azerbaijan falling apart into a myriad of tiny principalities. An attempt at unification was made by Fatalikhan of Kubá—he united the north-western principalities including Baku, and gravitated towards Russia, but after his death his efforts came to nought, and Azerbaijan was once again put at the mercy of conquerors. The country was bled by war. It needed protection. Now it looked more and more often to the north for help, to the growing power of Russia that had spread to the Caspian coast.

In 1806 Russia annexed a number of Azerbaijan principalities and Baku. The Russian victories over Persia were followed by the Gulistan and Turkmanchai peace treaties dividing Azerbaijan between tsarist Russia and Persia. The border running down the Araks river, became a border between blood brothers. It was a tragedy, but despite tsarist colonial policy there is no doubt that unity with Russia stimulated the economic, political and cultural development of the country. This is particularly true in the case of Baku.

An Oil Capital

"The name of that city will hardly appeal to the reader's curiosity," Jules Verne wrote in one of his novels. True, Baku was little known to the Europeans in the middle of the 20th century and not even that brilliant writer of science fiction was able to foresee its future.

At this time Baku was still a fortress-town on the coast, somewhat diminished after all the vicissitudes it had gone through. Merchants still put up at its many caravanserais. It still had a multitude of shops, but was now a transit market place: visitors exceeding the local population of under six thousand. The latter was made up of artisans, inn-keepers, tea- and shish-kebab-shop owners, bath attendants, barbers and of the other service trades of the time, plus the peasants who tended the gardens and grazed the flocks outside the city walls. The Maiden Tower, a few mosques and other relics of the city's former greatness overlooked a sea of low flat-roofed houses.

By the mid-19th century a viceroy had been installed in

Entrance to the Shirvan-Shahs' Palace.

View of *Gyz Galassy* (Maiden Tower).

the Caucasus and Baku included within the Shemakha gubernia (administrative region). In 1859 a devastating earthquake razed Shemakha to the ground and its function of centre was for the third, and last, time transferred to Baku.

That called forth some administrative and private building. The fortress lost its defence value and by 1867 was abandoned which led to a building boom—stone houses of the European type started to be built outside its walls.

The advantages of Baku's geographical position as a meeting-place of trade routes from Russia, Persia, Central Asia and the Caucasus, and above all of its oil, came again to the fore.

World economic development sharply raised demand for oil. As a result of Azerbaijan's unity with Russia, Baku was now involved in Russia's rapid industrial growth. In 1823 the first paraffin plant in the world was built to process the Baku oil. A little later the world's first deep borehole was drilled at the old oil-field of Bibi-Eibat not far from Baku. One of the world's earliest oil plants, built to the design of the famous German chemist Liebig, was put up near the ancient fire-worshippers' temple in Surakhany.

A new period began in 1872 when lease by tender was substituted for the former system of commission which had given incentive to trade but not to extraction. The rush

was on: to drill, strike oil, make a fortune... The only parallel to the Baku oil rush is the gold rush at Clondike. At the beginning of the century over half the world's oil came from Baku.

The world's oldest pipe-lines, railway tankers, and tanker ships appeared here. Within a short time one of the largest shipping companies in Russia had been set up in Baku, a telegraph organized and a railway built. No other town in Russia experienced such quick growth rates as Baku, which came to be known as an "American style" city. The following table gives an idea of the dynamic growth of its population which increased a hundred times over a hundred years:

```
1874—    15,000
1897—   112,000
1920—   313,000
1939—   791,000
1959—   987,000
1982— 1618,000
```

Construction was haphazard with no regard for urban harmony, profit being the only concern. A contemporary journalist wrote, "I see Baku as a grim-faced businessman up to his neck in accounts with no thought to spare for greenery, beauty or poetry." Greenery apart, there was a shortage of drinking water, no sewage system, and transport was outdated...

This is what Gorky says: "All day, from morning to night, I walked round the wells, half out of my mind with the oppressive heat and a persistent cough..." And another Russian writer, Alexander Grin: "I was once at Balakhany oilfields, job-hunting with another couple of down-and-outs and left it with relief—the black derricks, empty lanes, and oil-soaked earth with not a blade of grass or a tree were morbid and nightmarish."

Baku was one of the first cities to face the 20th-century problem of pollution. Despite the negative side effects of buoyant industrial growth, the city soon became a major centre of the Russian Empire. That same growth stimulated an unprecedented rate of urban development.

The modest provincial empire style buildings of the mid-19th century were followed by more imposing ones. Their architecture expressed the spirit of the time—gone was the fear of invasion, the medieval walls and fences were pulled down, houses with wide windows now faced the street. Windfall fortunes plus Caucasian temperament sometimes resulted in rather startling eclectic architecture, but there were more and more really fine buildings in the best national tradition going up.

In 1898 a survey of the city was carried out under the direction of von der Nonne and the First Master Plan drawn up.

Path of Progress

From the mid-19th century, as a result of the impact of Russian culture, the democratic trends of the 1860s and the fact that Azerbaijan young men were now being educated at Russian universities, Azerbaijan culture underwent a fundamental change. This expressed itself in new ideas and genres, new spiritual values and a new concern for civic responsibility.

By linking its history with Russia, and thus with Europe, Azerbaijan, while retaining its eastern roots and sharing its heritage with others, was one of the first countries of the Islamic world to absorb the ideological and aesthetic values of the new age and embark on the path of progress.

Thanks to Friedrich Bodenstedt's translations of the poetry by the "wise man of Ganja", Mirza Shafi, became known in Europe. An interesting study of Azerbaijan history was written by Abbas Kuli-aga Bakihanov, one of the new generation of national intellectuals having both an oriental and European education. Outstanding among the latter is Mirza Fatali Akhundov, the first Moslem writer of comedies, educator and public figure. He was the first oriental materialist philosopher who was deeply influenced by Russian literature and the struggle of the Russian democrats against serfdom and tzarist despotism. Akhundov's *Eastern Poem* written on the occasion of Pushkin's death (1837) struck readers by the depth of its feeling.

1873 marks the opening of the Azerbaijan national theatre with a production of an Akhundov's comedy. In 1875 Hassan-beck Zardabi, a leading publicist and public figure started publishing the first national newspaper *Akinchi* (Ploughman) in Baku. 1908 saw the first night of Uzeir Hadjibeckov's opera "Layla and Majnun", the first opera in the Eastern world. Educational establishments, charities and societies sprang up in Baku one after another. In 1894, Nariman Narimanov founded the first public library. Of particular importance in the development of social thought at the time was the *Mullah Nasreddin* magazine, founded and edited by Djalil Mamedkulizade, the outstanding author, dramatist and journalist. Among the intellectuals grouped round the magazine were Sabir and Azim Azimzade famous for their satirical sketches, verses and cartoons.

Revolutionary Struggle

The capitalist development of Baku gave birth to the industrial proletariat. Labour was attracted to the city from the Azerbaijan villages, from all over Russia, from abroad. Whereas in the early 19th century the population was mostly engaged in agriculture and small-time trade, by 1917 Baku had a 100,000-strong industrial labour force with a total population of 300,000.

Ruthless exploitation, pittance wages, life in the crowded barracks built on the oil-soaked land next to the derricks, shortage of water, even of drinking water, and other privations led to rising unrest. Strikes over economic issues acquired an increasingly political character. An active part was played by the Russian Social-Democrats.

The early 20th century saw unprecedented dramatic events significant not only for Baku but for the whole of

Russia. In 1901 a Leninist branch of the Social-Democratic party was formed and an underground printing press, known as "Nina", started. In 1902 the first political demonstration was held in Baku, and in 1903 the first general strike, news of which reverberated throughout the Caucasus, the Ukraine and Southern Russia. In 1904 the so-called "oil constitution", the first collective agreement in the history of the Russian working-class movement was concluded with the management. A group of Bolshevik orientation, the "Gummet" (Energy) was organized. In 1905 the first Baku Soviet (Council) of Workers' Deputies was set up and in 1906—the Trade Union of Petroleum Producing Workers. The revolutionary flame kindled in Baku was not to be forgotten in Russia and the East despite the defeat of the Russian 1905-1907 revolution. "In 1908, Baku gubernia topped the list with 47,000 strikers. The last of the Mohicans..." Lenin wrote.

The Baku Commune

In February 1917 the tsarist government fell. In October a meeting of the Baku Soviet which was attended by members of the public gave a welcome to the Great October Revolution in Petrograd. In April 1918 the Council of People's Commissars was formed following the suppression of an anti-Soviet rising. It was in this very complex situation, with the neighbouring regions in the hands of the counter-revolution, that the Baku Commune was set up— the first "oasis of the Revolution" in the Caucasus and the Eastern world. It issued decrees nationalizing land, the oil industry, the mercantile marine, etc., which were enthusiastically supported by thousands of Baku's workers and despite the famine and disruption fostered by external and internal enemies it won the people's trust for the Bolsheviks.

Fearing that the Soviet power would spread from Baku to other parts of Azerbaijan the enemies of the revolution set up the so-called Trans-Caucasian Sejm (Assembly) which approached the German and Turkish troops with the request for help. In July 1918, German troops occupied Georgia and Turkish—Armenia; they entered Azerbaijan and threatened Baku. Volunteer Red Army units managed to contain their offensive. At the same time British troops stationed in Iran negotiated with the Baku Social-Revolutionary, Dashnak (nationalist) and Menshevik Social-Democratic parties, a political bloc which succeeded in pushing through the Baku Soviet a resolution that the British be invited to "defend" the city from the Turkish invasion. The leaders of the Baku Commune condemned this action as treason and resigned from the government refusing to cooperate with the occupiers. The British landed in Baku, but, as predicted by the Bolsheviks, far from trying to defend the city from the Turks, they left it within a month, having disarmed the Soviet troops and executed by firing squad 26 leaders of the Baku Commune: 7 government members, headed by Shaumian, and 19 Soviet, Party and military activists, known as 26 Baku Commissars. The British also carried off a large part of the city's oil reserve.

28th of April

Power in Baku was now in the hands of the counter-revolutionary bourgeois nationalist Mussavat (Equality) party, which set up a government. The ensuing repressions, however, failed to curb the struggle waged by the workers of Azerbaijan for justice and freedom. The economic crisis, rising famine and poverty led to the growth of the revolutionary movement. Under Bolshevik leadership the new wave of strikes became increasingly organized. More and more calls were heard at workers' meetings that Azerbaijan join Soviet Russia. An underground shipping-line functioned between Baku and Astrakhan that heroically, in inadequate vessels, supplied Russia with oil and Baku revolutionary movement with money and arms...

In February 1920, at a congress held illegally in Baku, the separate Bolshevik groups in the city were united into the Communist Party of Azerbaijan. That historic event was to play a decisive part in further developments.

The Baku Commune tragedy, as well as later attempts by the Communists to cooperate with the Social-Revolutionaries and other parties, proved such cooperation to be impossible. Just as the SRs plus the local nationalists betrayed the Communists in Baku by giving the city up into the hands of the interventionists, in July 1918 the SRs, having entered into a coalition government with the Bolsheviks, staged an armed uprising in Moscow. In this way the parties of the petty bourgeoisie compromised themselves and lost all political influence, while the Communist Party, representing the interests of the working people became, and still is, the sole leader of Soviet society. A one-party system in Azerbaijan, as in other republics of the USSR, is the result of objective historical development.

The Ist Congress of the Communist Party of Azerbaijan began preparing for an armed uprising with the aim of overthrowing the Mussavat government. Red Army units were formed, a naval force under the command of Chinghiz Ildrym, a Bolshevik, controlled Baku port. The Mussavat government, faced with an ultimatum, resigned, but threatened to blow up the oil installations. To avert that danger the Baku Bolsheviks appealed to the Soviet government for urgent help. On April 28, 1920 the first armed train of the 11th Army entered Baku meeting no resistance. A monument in Tbilisskoye Shosse commemorates the event. Thus Soviet power was finally established in Azerbaijan.

Following the establishment of Soviet power in neighbouring Georgia and Armenia, a treaty was concluded in March 1922, setting up a Federative Union of Socialist Trans-Caucasian Republics, which was soon transformed into a united Trans-Caucasian Soviet Federative Republic.

In December of the same year the Trans-Caucasian Republic together with the Ukraine, Byelorussia and the Russian Federation united to form the Union of Soviet Socialist Republics (USSR). According to the new 1936 USSR Constitution Azerbaijan, Georgia and Armenia became separate constituent republics of the Soviet Union.

Socialist Construction

From the earliest days of Soviet power the Revolutionary Committee, and later the Council of People's Commissars, chaired by Nariman Narimanov (later Chairman of the Trans-Caucasian Federation and Co-chairman of the Central Executive Committee), embarked on a programme of peaceful construction which transformed all aspects of life in Baku. This took the form of the nationalization of industry, land, railways, banks, etc. New, well-appointed townships for the oil workers were built all over Apsheron, despite shortages of materials and the hard times. In May 1921 Lenin expressed particular concern for Baku's development.

The rehabilitation of industry, particularly of oil production, was hampered by the disruption caused by the Civil War, foreign intervention and underground counter-revolutionary activity. In April 1922 saboteurs set fire to the Surakhany oil installations. The blaze was put out by workers and engineers who received a cable from Lenin thanking them for their heroism and self-sacrifice at a time of extreme danger.

The disruption was overcome, the oil plants and other industries restored. New installations were put into operation, among them the first sea platforms. Baku's factories produced new types of drills and pumps; here too the Soviet Union's first iodobromide plant and new refining capacities were built. In 1926 the first electric railway in the USSR, running from Baku to the Apsheron oil-fields, was opened.

Theatres and libraries were opened to the public at

large, and a Society for Azerbaijanian studies founded. New schools, training colleges, higher education establishments and research laboratories came into being. As everywhere in the USSR the majority of the population was taught to read and write. The replacement of the difficult Arabic alphabet alien to Azerbaijan phonetics by first the Latin, and then the Russian alphabet cannot be overestimated for it introduced thousands of working people to the treasures of Russian and world culture.

The city was modernized and developed: its overall layout, architectural ensembles and central streets were taking shape, the public utilities were put in order. Whole new districts were laid out consisting of attractive modern buildings, monuments and gardens. Henri Barbusse wrote: "If I were asked to name a Soviet achievement that would strike both friends and even enemies of the USSR, I would say—look at Baku." Maxim Gorky said: "Baku is hard to recognize: very little is left of the former chaotic gray mass of houses similar to the heap of ruins left in the wake of an earthquake. Wide new streets have been laid out, the gray stone is graced by greenery, the trees of the seaside Primorsky Boulevard have grown wonderfully, the tram-cars roll gayly back and forth. I saw the city at night from a hill which is to be the site of the Botanical Gardens and was amazed by the beauty of the blazing lights..."

The further development of the city envisaged by the Second Master Plan of 1937 was interrupted by the vicious attack of Nazi Germany. Like the rest of the Soviet people the citizens of Baku had to take up arms. Women, children and old people went to work in the oil plants substituting for the men at the front. Despite the difficulties with supplies and the fact that women made up one third of the labour force, the country's "oil furnace" proved itself once again to be up to the mark: during the war Baku accounted for 70 per cent of the country's oil production, for about 90 per cent of its aircraft fuel.

Extraction as well as delivery was a problem. With the northern part of the Caucasus occupied by the

Nazis oil had to be delivered via the Caspian and Central Asia. Railway tankers were towed on floats across the sea, put back on rails the other side of the Caspian and sent to the front.

After the victory over the Nazis and post-war rehabilitation Baku went back to its development programmes... Off-shore oil production was pioneered on a large scale: on 7 November, 1949 the Oil Rocks sea platform township 70 miles off the shore began operations. Baku was the first place in the Caucasus to manufacture pre-fab housing: the pre-cast panel plant which went into operation in 1960 made possible the development of new districts housing hundreds of thousands of people.

Baku Today

In the 1970s Azerbaijan became the biggest producer of grapes in the USSR—its grape crop being equal to that of the other Caucasian republics and the Russian Federation put together; and a major producer of cotton, vegetables, tea, tobacco, citrus fruit, saffron, olives, pomegranates, nuts, etc. Agricultural growth stimulated the food and canning industry. A champagne factory was built in Baku.

Azerbaijan is a major Soviet manufacturer of oil products, steel pipes, non-ferrous metals, synthetic rubber, electric engines, automobile tyres, mineral fertilizers, building materials, electrothermic equipment, china and earthenware, carpets, textiles, wool, cotton and natural silk. It accounts for 70 per cent of Soviet oil-producing equipment, and most of the air-conditioners made in the country; 360 items are exported to 80 countries. Despite efforts at decentralization, to foster industry in the other cities of Azerbaijan, almost half of the above mentioned goods are made in Baku.

Baku today is known not only for its oil and petrochemical industry, but also for its electrical, mechanical and radio engineering, electronics, tele-communications, and machine tools industries. New industries speeding up the technological revolution account for over one third of its industrial structure, but this is not to say that the extraction industry is decreasing in importance: oil extraction is four times that of 1920, gas production is also on the increase. The latest subsea technology is used, including cable drilling.

The scale of open-sea oil exploration and extraction in the Caspian made it necessary to set up a yard for building deep-sea platforms (weighing up to 20,000 tonnes

Part of the Sumgait plant, one of the biggest industrial complexes in Azerbaijan.

Akhundov State Public Library.

each)—the only one of its kind in the USSR. These platforms which are delivered to site by special dump-barges are the size of a football pitch. Still newer methods for oil extraction are being researched.

A long-term development plan for Greater Baku has been drawn up to the year 2000. Baku combines three characteristics making for dynamic growth—a capital city, it has an advanced industry plus rich natural resources. In the near future Greater Baku will absorb towns within a 70-mile radius of the city. Trees will be planted over 15 per cent of the area of Greater Baku.

The inner city is also being replanned: new buildings include hotels such as the Moskva and Karabakh, Gulistan restaurant, a new cultural centre, the Youth Centre, an attractive marriage registrar's office, a new market, *Sherg Bazary*, new department stores, schools, shops, hospitals, etc. A ring road and motorways have been constructed to ease the traffic. The water supply is improved due to the construction of a new pipeline from the Kura river. Housing construction is constantly growing—every fifth citizen has recently moved to a new house.

Baku has become an important educational and research centre: virtually all of Azerbaijan's university-level educational establishments and research institutions are

At the international youth camp outside Baku.

One of the townships for the deep-sea oil-workers.

More grapes are grown in Azerbaijan than anywhere else in the USSR.

to be found in the capital. Graduates from dozens of countries have received a higher education in Baku.

Baku is sometimes referred to as an "oil academy" for its achievements in fundamental research in that field and some technical breakthroughs, such as turbine drilling, cementation of oil-wells, obtaining synthetic rubber from natural gas. Visitors from all over the USSR and from abroad come here for advice and consultations. Baku experts have contributed to oil exploration both in the Soviet Union and abroad, as well as to the theory and practice of the petrochemical industry. Azerbaijan scientists and scholars have achievements to their credit in physics, mathematics, astrophysics, geology, biology, christallography and Oriental studies. Baku has also won recognition for its combined research and production aero-space centre, the first to be built in the USSR, which has turned out some valuable equipment and systems for use both on earth and in space, particularly for the exploration of natural resources by remote-control sounding.

With over 180 libraries, 30 museums, more than 100 clubs and six theatres, Baku has a rich and varied cultural life. Among the best cultural facilities are: the Azizbeckov Drama Theatre (the oldest in the city), the Vurgun Russian Drama Theatre which performs in Russian, the

Akhundov Opera and Ballet Theatre, whose ballet company won the gold medal at the 6th Festival of Dance in Paris in 1969, the Magomayev Philharmonic Society. The State Symphony Orchestra, the State Dance Ensemble, the State Theatre of Song (one of its kind in the USSR) created by the famous singer Rashid Beibutov, the *Gaya* ensemble—won popularity throughout the country. The *hanendé* concerts given by the *ashugi*—performers of a specific genre of folk music *mugam*—always attract a good audience, especially Zeinab Hanlarova's group, well-known in the other Caucasian republics as well as in the Near and Middle East.

Poetry reigned supreme in Azerbaijan art as late as the 19th century. The classical *beitas* were set to *mugam* music, manuscripts of poetry were illuminated by miniatures, carpets and other objects of applied art carried motifs from Nizami and Fisuli. Though today poetry shares its popularity with the other arts, the Day of Poetry (dedicated to the works of Nizami, Sabir, Fisuli, Vaghif and Samed Vurgun) still arouses great enthusiasm. Every autumn there is a Sergei Yessenin festival in the village of Mardakyany where the Russian poet wrote his "Persian" cycle.

The national Azerbaijan-Film studios produces feature films, popular-science films and documentaries many of

which have won acclaim all over the Soviet Union. Here the best Soviet and foreign films are dubbed into Azerbaijani. Baku has a radio station and a TV studio.

Over 200 periodicals are published in the republic with a total circulation of about 4.5 million. The national dailies are *The Communist* (in Azerbaijani), *The Baku Worker* (in Russian), in addition to several evening newspapers, papers aimed at young people plus papers specializing in literature, agriculture, sport, etc., all published in Baku.

Thousands of Baku inhabitants (a fifth of the total population) go in for sports and physical training. Sport attracts people of all ages, as visitors to the city can see for themselves by calling in at the "health zone" on the seafront Primorsky Boulevard.

Great importance is attached to the health service. The urological clinic, provided with the latest equipment, conducts important research and admits patients from Azerbaijan, as well as from neighbouring regions of the country. Baku has over 90 hospitals, and 40 sanatoria, pensions and rest homes, where, as is the case all over the USSR, the cost of accommodation and treatment is either fully or partially covered by the trade unions. There are 71 doctors and 122 nurses per 10,000 of the population. All medical care is free.

Zeinab Hanlarova—one of the most popular performers of *mugam*—and her group.

Typical scene reminiscent of Old Baku.

Prospekt Neftyanikov with the Azerbaijan Hotel in the background.

Baku is a major transport junction. Azerbaijan has 750 miles of railway. Suburban trains carry about 150,000 commuters a day. There are flights from Baku's Bina airport to more than 70 cities of the USSR. Ships of the Caspian Fleet call at 125 ports in 30 foreign countries. The Baku-Krasnovodsk ferry service cuts from three to three thousand miles (eight to twelve days' travelling time) off the journey from the European part of the USSR to Central Asia.

Baku maintains friendly relations with a number of twin cities in other countries—Dakar, Naples, Basra, Houston, Bordeaux and Sarayevo. In 1982 the tenth anniversary of Baku's friendly links with Naples was celebrated in both cities which have many points in common in so far as geographical lay-out, local flora and fauna and their people are concerned.

Business and cultural links help the twin cities to solve problems relating to ecology, transport, technical facilities, sports, medical care, etc. Thus, the Dakar town authorities drew on Baku's experience in the organization of infant and primary schools and also, in the provision of free hospital treatment.

✱ ✱ ✱

Dear visitors, Baku treasures your friendship. We hope that this brief acquaintance with the city's geography, history and present-day life will help you to get the most out of your excursions and walks round the city, out of your contacts with its people.

As to the three torches in Baku's coat of arms, they may be interpreted as follows: first—as the ancient "land of flames", second—as the eternal flame of memory in honour of the 26 Baku Commissars and those who gave their lives in the struggle against the fascists, and third—as the flame in the hearts of the people of Baku, a huge modern town where life is both dynamic and creative.

Tours Round Baku

ROUND TOUR

Route: 26 Commissars' Memorial—Hadjibeckov Conservatoire—Lenin Palace of Culture—Central Farmers' Market—Memorial Museum of the Underground Revolutionary Printing-Press "Nina"—Spartak Stadium—Akademgorodok (Academy of Sciences district)—Moskva Hotel—Kirov Park—USSR Friendship Society—Azneft Square—Intourist Hotel—Puppet Theatre—Samed Vurgun Memorial Flat—Musical Comedy Theatre—Historical Museum—Baku Branch of the Central Lenin Museum.

A combined trolley-bus and walking tour round the central part of the city which will take you up to the Nagornoye *(Mountain)* Plateau and down to the seafront.
Time: from 2.5 to 3 hours. This tour is best done be-

View of Baku bay.

tween 10 a.m. and 5 p.m.—to avoid morning and evening rush hours.

The starting point—Ploshchad Dvadtsati Shesti Bakinskikh Komissarov *(26 Baku Commissars Square)* is next to the Azerbaijan and Apsheron hotels, the largest in Baku, where foreign tourists are most likely to stay. Should you happen to be staying in one of the smaller hotels—the Intourist or Moskva—the starting point is easy to find, as all four hotels are connected by circle trolley-bus route 8. To reach this route turn left on leaving the Azerbaijan Hotel, cross Ulitsa Shaumiana *(Shaumian Street)*, and turn right into Ulitsa Leitenanta Shmidta *(Lieutenant Schmidt Street)*.

You are now at the head of Ulitsa Leitenanta Schmidta.

The street is named after Lieutenant Pyotr Schmidt (1867-1906) of the Black Sea Fleet who headed the uprising on the *Ochakov* cruiser in Sevastopol during the 1905-1907 revolution. The uprising was ruthlessly suppressed and its leaders, members of the local Soviet and Lieutenant Schmidt, were executed.

The corner building on the right is the **State Pedagogical Institute**, one of the first educational establishments set up in Baku under Soviet government (1921) to meet the urgent need for teachers necessitated by the campaign against illiteracy. It was originally built in 1913 as a

26 Baku Commissars' Memorial.

commercial school by the architect G. Termickelov. Over the years the institute has expanded: about 10,000 students are now taught at its 11 departments. The traditional disciplines (Azerbaijan language and literature, mathematics, physics, chemistry, biology) have been supplemented by art and music. That has required a new block which stands next to the old building. A plaque on the wall of the institute assembly hall, which used to be one of the largest in the city, commemorates a public recital here by poet Vladimir Mayakovsky.

Across the street is the **Dzerzhinsky Club**, one of the city's larger public buildings used for meetings, conferences, etc. It was built in 1953 by the architect G. Medjidov. In the classical style with imposing columns it contains a large (1,000 seats) and smaller auditoriums, a public library, a music school and rooms suitable for various pursuits and hobbies. Walk down the street past the Dzerzhinsky Club to the intersection with Ulitsa Hadjibeckova *(Hadjibeckov Street)* and you will come to one of the best-known sights of the city—Ploshchad Dvadtsati Shesti Bakinskikh Komissarov. For the best view of the square, turn left, walk down a block to reach the main entry to it, opening from Ploshchad Kirova *(Kirov Square)*. You will pass the local Soviet (Council) and the district Communist Party Committee. The whole district, as well as the underground

station in the square, bears the name of 26 heroes of the Baku Commune.

The station with exits onto Prospekt Kirova *(Kirov Avenue)* and Ulitsa Hadjibeckova is decorated with red smalt mosaic tiles after the method invented two hundred years ago by the Russian scientist Mikhail Lomonosov. It has a bas-relief representing the Baku Commissars.

You now face **Ploshchad Dvadtsati Shesti Bakinskikh Komissarov.** On the right you see a red granite stele with a high relief of the Baku Commissars by the well-known Soviet sculptor Sergei Merkurov, the author of many monuments and pieces of sculpture in Moscow (including Lenin's statue in the Grand Kremlin Palace). Starting work on his relief in 1924, Merkurov took nearly 25 years to complete it. He bequeathed it to the state with the request that it be put up in Baku. This was done in 1958. The relief is a monumental representation of the tragic scene: the figures facing the firing squad express courage, moral conviction, undaunted spirit and faith in their cause.

This dignified small square lined with greenery combines intimacy with a feeling of open space. At the turn of the century it was a vacant lot used for tethering horses. The square was laid out with busts of the 26 Commissars and a big pool (still to be seen today) after the establishment of Soviet power. During the 1st Congress of the Peoples of the East, held in Baku in 1920, the bodies of the 26 Commissars were moved from their first burial place (on the other side of the Caspian where they were executed) and reburied in the square.

Later the present memorial was constructed. It consists of a granite figure of a worker with head lowered in mourning, who holds a torch with the eternal flame in his outstretched palms. The white marble ring surrounding the memorial symbolizes the unity of the heroes of the Baku Commune. The ring rests on four granite supports as if on the shoulders of the four leaders of the Commune: Stepan Shaumian, Meshadi Azizbeckov, Aliosha Djaparidze and Ivan Fioletov. Their faces in metal bas-relief can be seen on the plain wall at the back of the square beyond the pool. The plainness of the wall is set off by the evergreen palms and flowers at its base. Every hour Requiem by the prominent Soviet composer Kara Karayev is transmitted through the loud-speakers within the marble ring.

The architects G. Aleskerov and A. Husseinov and sculptors N. Mamedov and I. Zeinalov, responsible for the memorial, were awarded a State Prize for it in 1972.

Thousands of people come here every year on 20th September to commemorate the anniversary of the tragic death of the 26 Baku Commissars.

Having paid your respects to the Commissars you may wish to visit the apartments, now **memorial museums, of Shaumian and Djaparidze**, as well as the **flat-museum of** the prominent Soviet leader **Sergei Kirov**. They all are in the vicinity of the square.

Having looked at the memorial turn left and walk in the direction of the imposing building housing the Republic's Library to the dental clinic where there is a stop of trolley-bus 8b.

Board the trolley-bus—the next stop is the **Hadjibeckov State Conservatoire** (on your left). In front of the conservatoire which combines elements of classical and national

Statue of Uzeir Hadjibeckov, the father of Azerbaijan classical music, in front of the entrance to the Conservatoire which bears his name.

architecture (architects S. Dadashev and M. Usseinov, 1936) is a monument (sculptor T. Mamedov, 1960) to the man who founded it in 1921 and after whom it is named— Uzeir Hadjibeckov, the father of Azerbaijan classical music. Over a thousand students—future composers, singers, instrumentalists, musicologists, some of them from abroad, study European and Oriental music at the conservatoire. The piano, violin and cello are taught along with national instruments such as the *tar, kemancha*, etc. The *hanendé* technique of singing is also taught. In one of the wings of the conservatoire there is an opera studio where students give productions of classical and modern works. The organ in the concert hall lends itself beautifully to the Azerbaijan *mugam* music.

Also on the left, behind a small garden with fountains is a concrete-and-glass building. This is the **Lenin Palace of Culture** (architects V. Shulgin and E. Melkhisedekov, 1972) where important meetings, conferences, symposiums and congresses are held. The main auditorium (2,000 seats) is also used for concerts, and has good acoustics.

On the right are two buildings standing side by side: the modern block of the new railway station and a building with a tower resembling a minaret, the former suburban Sabunchinski Railway Station.

Lenin Palace of Culture.

Further on, on either side of the street are two modern aluminium-and-glass buildings: on the left—is Azgosproyekt, the state organization responsible for research and development, on the right—the honeycomb façade of the Construction Bank.

The trolley-bus climbs a hill, turns left and then right into Ulitsa Sameda Vurguna *(Samed Vurgun Street)*, one of the busiest thoroughfares in Baku. Get off here to visit the largest market in the city and some other places of interest. A stall next to the bus stop sells mineral water. Thirsty tourists can try "Badamly" or "Syrab", the most popular kinds.

This part of Baku used to be a suburb where artisans and small-time traders lived. It was called *kiarpich-bassan* (the brick-yard). Bricks and kitchen crockery used to be sold here in the streets. It was also known for its refuse heaps. When it rained, the steep streets turned into dirty torrents of clay and rubbish. The *ambali* (porters) used to turn up their trousers and make an extra penny by giving piggy-back rides to passers-by...

Now cross the street to the **Central Collective Farmers' Market**, where the peasants sell their produce and then do their shopping in the state supermarket for manufactured goods next door. The market, built in the Soviet period, lies on several levels connected on both sides by wide flights of steps. Trading is done in covered as well as open-air stalls. According to the season, we recommend the famous Apsheron figs, *shaani* grapes, a particularly sweet variety, as well as pomegranates, quince, persimmon... Don't miss the many local herbs and spices: different varieties of pepper, mint, basil, saffron, coriander *(kinza)*, wild onions, tarragon *(tarkhun)*, barberries, etc., plus the dried fruits, essential ingredients of the Azerbaijan pilaff.

The peasants sell their private produce at the market as well as products representing payment in kind from the collective farm for their work (supplementing monetary remuneration). There are also co-operative and state stalls with fixed (though seasonally adjusted) prices. The long-term development plan for the city envisages the building of a new market on this site plus a shopping centre and a hotel.

Leave the market by the opposite gate and walk along Pervaya Iskrovskaya Ulitsa to No. 102, the memorial museum of the underground revolutionary printing-press "Nina". The press had its premises here from 1903 to 1906 when it was moved to St. Petersburg on the decision of the Central Committee of the Russian Social-Democratic Workers' Party. The exhibits include the press, some of Lenin's letters and some publications printed here: issues of the underground newspaper *Iskra* and the Georgian newspaper *Brdzola*, as well as Bolshevik pamphlets and leaflets. The press, hidden in a nondescript house in a Baku suburb, issued over a million and a half publications. The police failed to track down its whereabouts...

Now go back through the market to Ulitsa Sameda Vurguna and get on the trolley-bus at the stop where you got off it.

On the right is Baku's **Circus** set up in 1945 on the basis of the popular national tight-rope walkers' and wrestlers' troupes. The present building seating 2,000 was built in 1967 (arch. E. Ismailov and F. Leontieva).

The next stop is by the **Blue Mosque**—taking its name from the colour of its dome—a functioning Sunnite mosque. A curious fact: one of the architects who designed the circus is the grandson of the master who built the mosque.

The Azerbaijan Constitution, like the constitutions of the sister republics, guarantees freedom of worship. Baku has Azerbaijan and Tatar mosques, two Orthodox and one Gregorian Christian churches, two synagogues, as well as Baptist and Molokan chapels.

On the left is Officers' Park and further on, on the right, is the **Children's Park** with various attractions. Opposite the latter is one of Baku's oldest research and development institutes which has designed a number of petrochemical plants in Baku and elsewhere in the USSR.

The trolley-bus now reaches a busy Ulitsa Bakihanova *(Bakihanov Street)*. On the right is an imposing apartment block known as "Artists' House". The main façade looks onto Children's Park. The architecture, combining classical and national styles, determines the character of the whole district.

The trolley-bus turns into the street near the **Richard Sorge monument** (sculptor V. Tsigal, 1981).

Richard Sorge was a Soviet secret agent born in Baku in 1895 where his father, German by nationality, worked in the oil-fields. His grandfather was a follower and close associate of Marx and Engels. His mother came from a Russian railway worker's family that lived near Baku. Later the Sorge family moved to Berlin. Richard Sorge, a Soviet citizen, was a member of both the Communist Party of the USSR and that of Germany. In the 1930–40s he lived in Germany, China and Japan under the cover of a German journalist and succeeded in obtaining highly classified information including the exact date of Germany's attack on the Soviet Union, plans for Japan's participation in the war, etc. His brilliance is attested by the excellent references given him by the German Ministry for Foreign Affairs only a month before his arrest. He was arrested in 1941 and executed in 1944 in Japan. Sorge was posthumously awarded the title of Hero of the Soviet Union.

Statue of Hero of the Soviet Union Mekhti Husseinzade.

The monument represents a bronze plaque on which, as though indented with bullet shots, is an outline of Sorge's features. A Japanese *sakura* (cherrytree) branch is a reminder of the scene of his undercover activities against fascism.

Continuing down Bakihanov Street, on the left is the Volodarski garment factory. On the right is an oblong garden with a **statue** in the centre of **Sevil Kazieva**, the first Azerbaijan girl to drive a cotton harvester. Since then thousands of women have followed suit and now account for a large proportion of the republic's tractor drivers.

As the trolley-bus turns into Tbilisskiy Prospekt *(Tbilisi Avenue)*, the long-distance bus terminal can be seen through the trees. In the centre of a small garden on a pedestal resembling a granite rock is a monument to the war hero, **Mekhti Husseinzade** (sculptor F. Abdurrahmanov, 1973).

Mekhti Husseinzade, awarded the title of Hero of the Soviet Union, was born in Baku and graduated from art school and the Institute of Foreign Languages. In the Battle of Stalingrad he was wounded and taken prisoner. He escaped and formed a POW detachment that joined a Yugoslav-Italian guerilla corps. Known as "Michaello", Husseinzade became a living legend. He was killed during one of his operations.

The statue portrays him in action, grenade in hand, rushing forward, his cape streaming behind him...

On the right is the **Spartak Stadium**. Further up Tbilisskiy Prospekt is a new **covered arena** with 12,000 seats, and a sports complex with a cycling track. Further up the Aquatic Sports Palace under construction.

The trolley-bus turns a corner and approaches Prospekt Stroiteley *(Builders' Avenue)*, a continuation of Ulitsa Bakihanova. On the left is the Nakhichevan Hotel (architect S. Amirov, 1960). In 1981 the hotel was redesigned and renovated. On the right half-worked stone blocks mark the site of an open-air studio for young sculptors.

Prospekt Stroiteley got its name from the massive housing development of the Nagornoye Plateau which began in the 1950s. Before then there were only a few isolated buildings here at the approaches to the city. The area beyond the Nakhichevan Hotel was known at the beginning of the century as *hassar* (fence), for it was here that the cattle were kept before being sold.

The trolley-bus now passes through Ploshchad Pyatidesyatiletiya Sovetskogo Azerbaijana *(50th Anniversary of Soviet Azerbaijan Square)*. The severe geometrical building on the right is the Central Statistical Board; next to it is Baku's first high-rise apartment block. In the garden on the left is a small bas-relief of the Azerbaijan poet, Mushfig.

Next comes the Sabir Pedagogical College. Founded in 1920, it played an important part in the mass literacy campaign and later became known for training teachers of Russian for non-Russian schools.

Azerbaijan, as all the other parts of the USSR, has a 10-year compulsory secondary education system. All education, including university, is free of charge. Teaching is done in Azerbaijani as well as in Russian and the other languages of the USSR. An article in the Azerbaijan Constitution states that Azerbaijani as the official language of the republic is to be used in state, public, cultural and educational institutions. The state is to take measures to encourage the development of Russian and other languages spoken by the local population. As the common language of the multi-national USSR Russian plays an important role in cultural exchange and establishing international links and, for this reason, particular importance has been attached to the teaching of Russian in recent years. For many Azerbaijanis it has become their second native language.

The trolley-bus turns into Prospekt Narimanova *(Narimanov Avenue)*. The garden on the left is to be extended to run throughout the whole city to approximately the starting point of the present tour, near the Sabunchinsky Railway Station. It will thus form another central boulevard lying parallel to Primorsky Boulevard.

Before us lies **Akademgorodok** *(Academy of Sciences district)*. We now come to the main building of the **Repub-**

lic's **Academy of Sciences** (M. Usseinov, 1955) which houses research institutes and social science departments. It is surrounded by 17 research and development institutes specializing in physics, energetics, the study of deep-sea oil and gas deposits, geology, chemical technology, non-organic and physical chemistry, etc. The inventions of Azerbaijan scientists have been patented in many countries, including the USA, FRG, Japan, France and Great Britain. About two thousand patents and licences have been taken out within the last decade.

Design bureaus and pilot production plants attached to the research institutes help to speed up the introduction of new technology into industry. The Institute of Physics, for instance, is the leading institution in the country specializing in selenium and tellurium research. Transistor equipment for micro- and optoelectronics have been designed there, in particular, lazers with variable frequencies. Institute scientists working in conjunction with medical specialists have proved and explained the stimulating effect of selenium on eyesight. The fast-cutting steel without molibden or tungsten developed at the institute is now in use in many plants in the country. Azerbaijan scientists develop joint projects with other CMEA countries, and co-operate with 530 laboratories and research centres of 50 countries.

Beyond Akademgorodok is the University town centred round **Kirov State University**, the first establishment of higher education in Baku. It was founded in 1919 due to persistent efforts on the part of national progressive intellectuals with help from their Russian counterparts. At first the University only had two departments: the department of medicine and the history and philology department. Today it has 11 departments and 94 teaching chairs, as well as preparatory courses for new students. The student body numbers about 12,000. Its teaching staff includes prominent scientists and scholars. The University's research laboratories and its student design bureau have some important inventions to their credit, while its school of mathematics, the schools of Azerbaijan linguistics, literature and history have gained a considerable reputation.

Links are maintained with Czechoslovakia, there are joint teaching and research programmes with France, the GDR, Italy, the USA, Yugoslavia and Iraq. The University press publishes works by faculty members and undergraduates, periodicals, etc.

The next large building along Prospekt Narimanova (also on the right) is the **Chinghiz Ildrym Polytechnic**, named after one of Azerbaijan's first engineers, a participant of the Great October Revolution in Petrograd, later a People's Commissar and a leading figure in the national economy. The Polytechnic was founded in 1950 on the basis of the Petrochemical Institute. It has 12 thousand students majoring in 23 subjects study at its 7 departments. The institute is organized into 41 chairs. It has a research laboratory, library, publishing house and printing press. During 1982 alone 30 patents and licences were taken out for the Polytechnic's inventions, four of them in the USA.

Recently four of the Polytechnic's departments and some specialized chairs were formed into a separate Civil Construction Institute, the 18th seat of higher education in

Main building of the Azerbaijan Academy of Sciences.

the republic. It will soon be moving into a new building behind the Polytechnic.

On the right, further down the avenue are two apartment blocks whose architecture reflects elements of the traditional national style. Next is a small covered market, with the Djafar Djabarly cinema and a cafe opposite. Among the old houses behind the cinema is the memorial **Djafar Djabarly house-museum**. Djabarly was one of Azerbaijan's leading writers and playwrights.

The trolley-bus circles round a square in the middle of which is a **monument to Meshadi Azizbeckov** (sculptor T. Mamedov), one of the Baku Commune leaders. Erected in 1976 on the 100th anniversary of Azizbeckov's birth, it portrays him speaking at a public meeting.

On the right the trolley-bus passes the **Cemetery of Honour** where some outstanding leaders, scientists, writers and artists are buried: Uzeir Hadjibeckov, the poet Samed Vurgun, the scientist Ussif Mamedaliev and others.

In the past this mountainous part of the city contained many cemeteries, some of them for the victims of the cholera epidemic which struck Baku and the whole of the Caucasus in the 1890s. Today there is a big hospital here. The

Part of the University.

Moskva Hotel situated in the upper part of the city.

two large blocks have balconies facing the sea which afford the patients fresh air and a magnificent view. The average rate of life expectancy has doubled thanks to an improved health service, higher living standards and cultural level, as well as the right guaranteed in the Constitution to paid holidays and old-age pensions. Azerbaijan, as we said above, is now known for the longevity of its inhabitants.

Alight from the bus at the Central Kirov Park (also known as Nagorny Park) at the end of Prospekt Narimanova. Before entering the park have a look at the square in front of it. Standing with your back to the park, on the right is the Moskva Hotel (architect M. Usseinov, 1977), one of the best in Baku. On the left is the **State Committee for Radio and Television**. The TV centre with its 310-metre tower is situated at the highest point of Baku's natural rock terrace. It broadcasts on four channels. Apart from the republican programme it transmits the 1st and 2nd all-Union programmes as well as an educational programme. It also transmits Intervision and Eurovision programmes.

Old residents remember the time when an old oil derrick on a hill served for a TV tower. The derricks come right up to the city here, and one of them having done its time in

the oil-field was given, as it were, a new lease of life.

Between the Moskva Hotel and the TV centre is the **Supreme Soviet of Azerbaijan**. This impressive building was designed by T. Abdullayev, H. Rahmanova, Yu. Kadymov and constructed in 1980. Under its dome is an assembly hall for 750 (including the Presidium) and a number of auxiliary premises. There are visitors' galleries. Adjoining the hall and facing the sea is the 12-floor wing accommodating the Presidium Office.

It is not professional politicians, but representatives of all strata of the population (and this applies to the Soviets of the other USSR republics) that make up the Supreme Soviet of the Azerbaijan Republic. Of its 450 members 165 (36.6%) are industrial workers and 135 (30%)—collective farmers or agricultural workers. There are also members representing the intelligentsia, Party, state, trade union and Komsomol (Young Communist League) workers and armed forces servicemen: 179 of the members are women; 112 (24.8%) are under the age of 30; 138 (30.6%) are non-Party members; 22 members have the title of either Hero of the Soviet Union or Hero of Socialist Labour, 314 have been awarded state orders or medals; 42 have academic degrees.

Let us enter now **Central Kirov Park**. Near the gate, on the left, there is a monument to General Azi Aslanov, Hero of the Soviet Union, an outstanding commander of tank troops during World War Two. On the right is a small souvenir shop.

Laid out over hills (by architect L. Ilyin, in the 1930s) the 100-acre park commands a good view of the city and bay. Its picturesque site is put to good advantage: trees and shrubs are kept low and the open-air theatre, cafe, reading pavilion, stalls and other buildings are placed so as not to obstruct the perspective. The lay-out is crowned by a towering **monument to Sergei Kirov** (sculptor P. Sabsai, 1939) with a flight of wide steps leading up to it. The bronze figure of Kirov is placed on a pedestal of red granite. The monument which rises from the soft contours of the hills can be seen from several parts of the city.

In 1980 as part of the 60th anniversary celebrations of Soviet Azerbaijan the **House of Friendship of the Peoples of the USSR** was opened next door to the Kirov monument. It has an exhibition illustrating the historical links between Azerbaijan and Russia and the contribution made to their development by Azerbaijan scholars, scientists, writers and educationalists.

Nizami portrays a Slavic girl in his poem *Seven Beauties*. In another poem *Iskendar-nama*, he gives a mass of information about Rus' which indicates that ancient contacts existed between the two nations before the 12th century. This is confirmed by historians and archaeologists. The Russian merchant Afanasy Nikitin who went to Persia and India in the 15th century described Baku with its "eternal flames" in his *Voyage Beyond Three Seas*. Interest in the Caucasus and in Azerbaijan in particular was reflected in Pushkin's *Travelling to Arzrum* and Lermontov's adaptation of the Azerbaijan *dastan* (folk ballad) *Ashug Garib*. The long-standing trade and economic links led to cooperation in science: the great chemist Mendeleyev, the well-known geologist Gubkin and other Russian scientists participated in the exploration and extraction of Baku's oil and in the development of its industry; the first Azerbaijan engineers, doctors, etc., were educated in Russia, while Azerbaijan scholars M. Topchibashev, M. Kazembeck and others helped to lay the foundation of Oriental studies in Russia.

There are many such examples of links between the two peoples. But the best pages in the history of friendship between the Azerbaijan and Russian peoples were written in the course of their common struggle for social justice.

The oil boom in Baku and the town's unprecedented growth attracted, as we said, migrants from all over Russia and from abroad (mainly from Iranian Azerbaijan). "The multi-national composition of the oil-industry labour force in Baku is unparalleled anywhere in Russia," commented the *Yoldash* (Comrade) newspaper at the beginning of the century. "It is the meeting place of the world proletariat."

Photocopies of issues of the Leninist newspaper *Iskra*

printed by the "Nina" press, documents relating to the life and work of the 26 Baku Commissars who included men of different nationalities, and other exhibits, illustrate the consolidation of the international Soviet brotherhood in the revolutionary struggle. There is a copy of the Russian Federative Republic decree signed by Lenin granting credits to the Soviet government of Azerbaijan. Next to it is a newspaper report about Azerbaijan sending aid to famine victims in Russia.

A large part of the display is devoted to the creation of the USSR—a living embodiment of Lenin's policy on the nationality issue. One of the rooms contain samples of produce from the 15 Union republics: wheat from the virgin lands of Kazakhstan, potatoes from Byelorussia, apples from Moldavia, high-grade cotton from Central Asia. Many exhibits (photographs, letters, works of art and literature) bear witness to Azerbaijan's flourishing economy, science and culture, as well as to the international traditions of Baku's working class. In the 1930s a talented Azerbaijanian engineer, Chenghiz Ildrym, was put in charge of the construction of the giant Magnitogorsk iron and steel plant in the Urals; in the 1950s another Azerbaijanian, Farman Salmanov, was among the prospectors, who discovered the rich Tyumen oil and gas deposits in Western Siberia. Azerbaijan experts also took part in the construction of the

Baikal-Amur Railway Line, and now they help with land reclamation in the Archangel region (North Russia). On the other hand, some projects in Azerbaijan, such as the Minghechaour hydro-power plant, or the new chemical- and metal-industry city of Sumgait, built from scratch in the steppe, the second largest industrial centre after Baku, or the large-scale Shamkhor hydro-power plant, now under construction, have been an all-Union effort. Economic cooperation is functioning between 45 cities and districts of Azerbaijan and 656 plants, factories, construction projects, collective and state farms all over the Soviet Union.

The exhibition at the House of Friendship is completed by a display demonstrating Azerbaijan's latest achievements and its international links.

On leaving the House of Friendship climb up to the viewing platform at the foot of the Kirov monument. From here there is a magnificent panorama of the city clinging to the bay in the shape of a horse-shoe. It has been described many a time as seen from this point. The Soviet writer Lydia Libedinskaya wrote: "The city is at your feet—cubic-shaped, with sharp edges, unlike any other in the world. Huge and strong, with flat roofs and steep streets, trimmed with the iron lace of the oil derricks lending the landscape an outlandish beauty. It's getting dark, the lights come on—a necklace of lights round the bay, col-

One of the squares in Prospekt Neftyanikov. The steps and cable car to Kirov Park start from here.

Primorsky Boulevard

oured lights flash on the derricks, from the top of the mountains, from the sea. The waves pick the lights up, rock them and multiply them and carry them off with their regular heavy beat."

This is a good moment to sort out the general lay-out of the city with the help of a map. Take your bearings from the coastline: the seafront Primorsky Boulevard runs the whole way along the bay. It has a pier jutting out into the sea. Beyond it, you can see the passenger seaport. Opposite the seaport the Azerbaijan Hotel is clearly visible. Behind it is Lenin Square with Government House. A busy thoroughfare, Prospekt Neftyanikov *(Oil Workers' Avenue)*, runs down from Lenin Square parallel to the seafront, round the hill you are standing on, past the dry docks, and off in the direction of Bayilov district. The quick way of reaching the avenue is by cable railway. You have, in fact, been touring the upper, north side of the city.

Now look to your left: not far below is an unusual white building with two minaret-like turrets and an open-air stage facing you—the Philharmonic Society. The maze of streets beyond, stretching to Prospekt Neftyanikov, is the Old City *(Ichery-Shekher)*, the historical centre of the city. Strange as it may seem this part of the huge city at your feet used to be the whole of Baku at the beginning of the last century. At the time it was a fortress-town with a pop-

ulation, according to the 1813 census of 1,892 or of 6,494 if one includes the outer settlement and the 37 villages of Apsheron.

To descend to the city walk down the steps from the monument or, better still, take a cable-car ride. The upper stop is a short way from here. The **cable railway**, built in 1960, is 510 yards long and the ride takes three and a half minutes.

The cable railway ends at Prospekt Neftyanikov in a small square with a bronze **figure of Bahram Gura**, a character from Nizami's poem *Seven Beauties*. Looking back at the Kirov Park from here there is a good view of Baku's biggest restaurant, the Gulistan, with a variety show.

Facing the prospect, on the right, next to the cable railway stop, is the Azerbaijan Intourist Agency and next to it the Intourist Hotel, designed by Academician A. Shchusev in the 1930s, whose best-known work is the Lenin Mausoleum in Moscow. This plain and functional building was one of the first Intourist hotels in the country. Opposite it is a covered stadium for hand games, the biggest in the Caucasus. To the left are big apartment blocks.

Take a trolley-bus for the last leg of the tour. Cross the street, turn left and walk a hundred yards to Ploshchad Az-

The frescoes in the foyer of the Puppet Theatre. (Photos are of exhibits in the Azerbaijan Historical Museum.)

neft *(Azneft Square)* where there is a trolley-bus 8b stop. (Nos. 1 or 4 will also do).

The only building in the square, built in 1896, in French renaissance style (architect P. Stern), prior to the Revolution was the residence of Baku's Governor; in Soviet time it was taken over by the Azerbaijan Nationalized Oil Industry Board, later known as Azneft, an organization responsible for oil extraction on land. The same building houses an all-Union organization responsible for sea platforms in the Caspian as well as for oil and gas drilling in the Baltic and Black seas.

Before you is **Revolution Garden** running along the old fortress wall. Behind you is the beginning of the seafront, do not miss the fountain with its elegant stylized swans...

The bus goes down Prospekt Neftyanikov. To the right is Primorsky Boulevard, to the left—apartment houses with shops on the ground floor. They are interrupted by a small lawn surrounding a tall, old tower. This is the famous **Gyz Galassy (Maiden Tower)**, a remarkable architectural monument. The rather pretentious house next to it was built by a wealthy citizen of Baku, Hadjinski. The tower as well as the horse-drawn cabs parked nearby provide a glimpse of Old Baku, of which you will see more later.

Get off the trolley-bus at the next stop by an attractive white building on the seafront (with the main façade overlooking Prospekt Neftyanikov). Formerly the Phenomenon cinema, built in 1908, this is now the **Shayig Puppet Theatre**, named after a well-known pedagogue and children's writer. It is worth sparing a minute to have a look at the murals on folk-tale themes in the foyer (by T. Narimanbeckov). Apart from its productions for children, which have been awarded international diplomas and prizes, the theatre also puts on satirical shows for grown-ups.

As your hotel is not far from here we suggest you do the rest of the route on foot. Cross the street by the subway. A few dozen yards ahead is the Caspian Steamship Line Office (Caspar House). The apartment block to the right was built for the steamship line employees. On the ground floor is one of the best polyclinics in the town.

In the middle of the last century, with the Caspian at its

highest level, a large part of the present seafront was under water. If the seafront is a fairly recent addition to Baku, the district east of the fortress fast acquired a European aspect at the turn of the century—this was where oil-well owners, bankers, many of them foreigners, had their houses. Today it is a quiet residential area with narrow, somewhat gloomy streets.

Passing Caspar House, go down Ulitsa Shaumiana. On the left, after a block, is a house with a bas-relief on it. This is where Samed Vurgun, a well-known Soviet Azerbaijan poet, once lived. His flat on the second floor has been turned into a **memorial museum**: some of the rooms have been left as they were when he lived here; the rest contain an exhibition devoted to his life, work and public activities.

A little further on, on the right, is the **Shikhali Kurbanov Musical Comedy Theatre** designed by I. Gosslavsky in 1904. The building was constructed on the money of the oil millionaire and patron of the arts Zeinalabdin Tagiyev. A plaque on the wall of the theatre (the original building designed by architect P. Kognovitski in 1899 was burnt down) tells us that this is where the first Azerbaijan opera "Layla and Majnun" was given its first production. It was written by Uzeir Hadjibeckov, the founder of the national school of musical comedy. Hadjibeckov's masterpieces "Arshin Mal Alan", "Meshadi Ebad" and others, form part of the theatre's repertoire.

Turn left into Ulitsa Malygina *(Malygin Street)*, named after one of the 26 Commissars—the corner building opposite is the **History Museum** (founded in 1920). The museum moved to its present home (formerly the Z. Tagiyev palace, built in 1898–1902 by I. Goslavski) in 1954.

> For the convenience of the visitor not going on a guided tour of the museum, we include here a brief guide to the contents of its rooms.

The Azerbaijan History Museum

Ground Floor. History and archaeology exhibition from antiquity to the 19th century.

Entrance Hall—a *kiup* pitcher (2 metres high) from the

Sary-tepe settlement (c. 10th–9th centuries B.C.).
Room 1 (right of Entrance Hall). From Stone Age to the 3000 B.C.
To the left of the entrance is a human jaw bone found in the Azykh cave. The archaeological finds there led to the study of the earliest on USSR territory, and one of the earliest in the world, Kuruchai culture. On the right are fossils from Binagali, the ancient oil lake near Baku; relics from Kobustan including the famous rock-carvings; petroglyphs from Apsheron and elsewhere in the republic.
Room 2. Bronze Age (c. 3000–1000 B.C.)

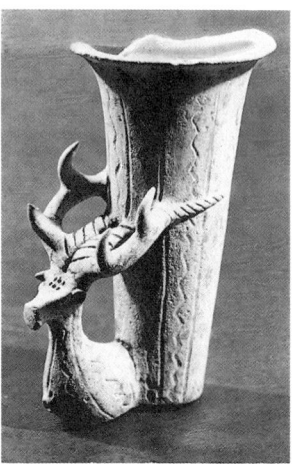

Decorated red clay vase. 1st millennium B.C.

Ritual vessel decorated with a deer's head, 1st-2nd centuries B.C.

Capital of a column from an ancient church decorated with two peacocks, a flower and an Albanian inscription.

Among the tools, implements, weapons and ornaments in the show-cases are: stone forms for bronze casting confirming the local origin of the latter items; boot-shaped ceramic vessels; a unique decorated red-clay vessel (Nakhichevan); a butter churn and jug decorated with an ear of wheat from the Khodjaly burial mound; a harness and equestrian decorations. Of great interest are: an agate bead with a cuneiform inscription mentioning the Assyrian King Adadnirari (pre 8th century B.C.), and a collection of Bronze Age beads, including beads made of shells. A model of a burial mound of the so-called "concealed burial" type, contains implements and tortoise shells (Minghechaour).

Room 3 (to left of entrance). Iron Age (early 1000 B.C.).

The items on view include: tools and weapons, household items, amulets and charms found in burial mounds dating back to the time of the first known states on the territory of Azerbaijan (10th–5th centuries B.C.); burial urns (early centuries A.D.); tombs (3th–9th centuries A.D.); a stone with a Latin inscription of the 1st century A.D. testifying to the presence of the Romans near Baku (Kobustan); a picture representing Alexander the Great meeting with Atropat. A separate show-case illustrating Azerbaijan's relations with the Hellenic world contains, among other items, the oldest collection of coins to have been found in Azerbaijan and examples of the first coins to have been minted in the country (3rd century B.C.). The so-called "Hynislin Statue", a solid rock idol, two metres high, dating back to the Zoroastrian period (1st century A.D.), was found near Shemakha. One of the most important exhibits—the archaeological stratigraphical sections taken from cultural deposits during excavations near Minghechaour—reflect the continuity of culture from earliest times to the late Middle Ages.

Also in this room are exhibits relating to the early Middle Ages (3rd–12th centuries). Among them are: a piece of ornamentation from a church (5th–6th centuries), showing two peacocks in relief with ribbons round their necks, a flower between them and a unique Albanian inscription running along the cornice in an alphabet formerly considered lost; examples of carving on stone, metal, wood and bone (3rd–7th centuries). Items found during excavations of early mediaeval Azerbaijan towns include a ceramic water supply pipe (Ganja, 10th century) and a kiln from Minghechaour (6th–7th centuries), pointing to the local origin of the majority of the earthenware. There is a collection of attractive glass vessels and silver cups from Kabbala, Minghechaour and Barda; hoards of Sassanide, Byzantine, Arab and local coins, the latter minted in 6th–7th centuries in Nakhichevan, Barda and other cities.

A special display in this room is devoted to the liberation struggle led by Javanshere and Babek against the Arab Caliphate.

Room 4. Azerbaijan culture, 11th–14th centuries.

The exhibits include: busts of the great men of Azerbaijan letters, art and science (the poet and philosopher Nizami Ganjevi, the architect Adjemi Nakhichevani, founder of the Nakhichevan school of architecture, the poetess Mekhseti, the astronomer Nasreddin Tussi, and others); their manuscripts; photographs of architectural monuments—fortresses, palaces, castles, mosques, tombs,

19th-century copper jug.

Glazed 17th–18th-century bowl decorated with a zebu.

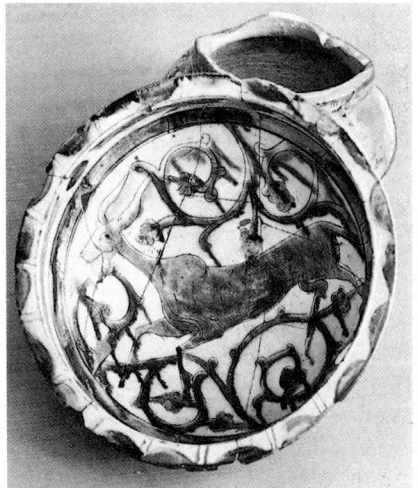

caravanserais; and a stone with a kufic inscription (12th century) found among the ruins of Baku's fortress wall.

The second section of the exhibition is devoted to the Mongol invasion. There is a painting of Shemakha after it had been taken by the Mongols and objects from warriors' graves in Minghechaour: examples of Mongol clothing, a birch-bark quiver, weapons, harness, fabrics, an envoy's credential *paiza*.

The third section relates to the 15th–17th centuries and consists of items dating back to the Azerbaijan states of Kara-Koyunlu, Ak-Koyunlu, of the Shirvan-Shahs and the Safevids. Among them are: household items of great artistic value, ink-wells, quilts, book-stands from the *mekteb* and *madrassah* schools, sports items of the period, beautiful local fabrics, a silver dish (16th cent.), collections of Azerbaijan copper and gold coins. On the left is a model of a typical house interior with separate quarters for men and women containing some period household objects, such as a hookah, bath shoes decorated with mother-of-pearl, etc. There are books by and portraits of the late Middle Ages poets—Fisuli, Nasymi, Shah Ismail (Hattai)—all of whom wrote in Azerbaijani.

At the far end of the room are examples of applied art and crafts—fabrics, carpets (18th cent.), silk garments, embroidery, musical instruments.

Room 5 (through a passage). Azerbaijan culture, 18th century.

On view are: examples of ornamental copperware (bowl, tray, etc.); flint-lock arms, sabres and daggers, some of them of Damascus steel from the Azerbaijan village of Laghich where they knew how to make this steel; small-scale models of a threshing floor with agricultural tools of the period and of artisans' shops.

There are photographs of architectural monuments, for instance of the Sheki Khans' Palace with its carved frames and stained-glass windows *(shebeke)* along the façade and wonderful wall paintings. Among the other items are works by the 18th-century poets Vaghif and Vidadi, khans' regalia including a Ganja Khan's staff, a Karabakh Khan's mace, and the tomb-stone of the latter; the cradle of Khan

Muhammad Hassan, encrusted with mother-of-pearl.

A separate display reflects relations and cultural links between Azerbaijan and Russia.

First Floor (left). From the 19th century to the present time.

Room 1. Azerbaijan becomes part of the Russian Empire.

The display starts off with a quotation from Engels on the progressive role played by Russia in the East.

The exhibits include: a painting (early 19th cent.) by F. Rubo depicting a scene from the Russo-Iranian war; standards of the khans; keys to the cities of Azerbaijan; Russian and eastern weapons and medals of the period, horse-drawn cannon, etc. General Paskevich's (commander of the Russian army in the Caucasus during the Russo-Iranian war) words about the courage of the Moslem (i.e. Azerbaijan) regiments are reproduced. The following items are shown together with a scale model of a peasant house: an imported lamp from Russia replacing the traditional ceramic *chirakh*; an Azerbaijan woman's dress made of Russian cotton, Russian imperial money and weights and measures of the time.

The remaining part of the room is devoted to Azerbaijan culture of the first half of the 19th century, to its most outstanding figures. A separate display case contains some personal effects of Mirza Fatali Akhundov and first editions of his works.

Rooms 2–5. Life in the countryside; the development of industry in the second half of the 19th and early 20th century.

Among the agricultural implements is a *dink* for threshing rice. There is a water-colour by A. Azimzade called "Tax Collecting by Beks and Clergy", peasant petitions complaining of injustice; weapons used by bands of escaped serfs in their struggle against the authorities.

There are many exhibits reflecting the development of towns—mainly Baku. These include samples of industrial goods produced by the first plants and factories; a photo of the world's first tanker—the *Zoroaster* (1878); a pail with a valve plus other tools used by the oil-worker, miner, and copper-smith; a silver plaque issued by the Nobel Bros in 1906 to mark the production of a billion poods of oil (a pood—36 lb.).

Rooms 6–7. Various documents pertaining to the spread of Marxism, the first Social-Democratic groups in Azerbaijan, the first instances of industrial workers' action. Mementoes of the labour movement and the first Russian revolution of 1905–1907 as well as of the Iranian revolution of 1905–1911.

Some of the exhibits reflect events in Azerbaijan after the February revolution: a photograph of the first session of the Baku Soviet (1917), portraits of its leaders, etc.

Room 8. Azerbaijan culture from the second half of the 19th century to the victory of the socialist revolution.

The objects presented illustrate the beginnings of the national press, theatre, professional music, realistic painting and sculpture. They include copies of the first issues of

V.I. Lenin Museum.

the *Ekinchi* newspaper and *Mollah Nasreddin* magazine; playbills of the first drama and musical productions; watercolours by Azerbaijan artists. Photos and personal possessions of outstanding figures in the arts: Natavan, Mamedkulizade, Zardabi, Sabir, Hadjibeckov, Magomayev, Arablinski, Kengerli, Azimzade, and others.

Room 9. Folk arts and crafts.

The items on display include: national costume made of embroidered velvet worn by the Azerbaijan women; examples of bead and gold embroidery, jewellery and carpets; ornamental copperware, etc.

The rest of the first floor is devoted to exhibitions on the history of Soviet Azerbaijan.

The first part of the display in these rooms relates to the triumph of the Great October Revolution, to the establishment of Soviet power in Baku, to the struggle against foreign intervention and the Mussavat government (1917-20). On view are the first decrees issued by the Baku Council of People's Commissars; Lenin's letters and other documents testifying to the assistance given by revolutionary Russia to the Azerbaijan proletariat. The history of the Baku Commune and the 26 Commissars is reflected in photographs, paintings, personal possessions, documents and other exhibits.

Items illustrating the triumph of the socialist revolution and socialist construction (1920-41) include: photos, weapons and personal possessions of the 11th Red Army men who supported the workers' uprising in Baku in 1920; documents testifying to the efforts of the Central Committee of Azerbaijan's Communist Party led by S. Kirov and the first Soviet government of Azerbaijan headed by N. Narimanov to mobilize the working force in order to overcome economic disruption, rehabilitate the republic's economy and ensure its development; the texts of the Azerbaijan Constitutions of 1921 and 1925.

There is graphic evidence of the popular enthusiasm during the first five-year-plan periods when new industrial centres were established, agriculture developed, and Azerbaijan was transformed from a backward province of the Russian Empire into an agro-industrial sovereign Socialist Republic. There are materials relating to the campaign against illiteracy, and to the setting up of secondary schools and establishments of higher education. Also on view is the text of the 1937 Constitution.

Various exhibits demonstrate Azerbaijan's contribution to victory in the Great Patriotic War of 1941-45. Among them are documents testifying to the heroic feats of the Baku oilmen who supplied ¾ths of the army requirements for fuel; materials relating to the battle for the Caucasus in which the 18th Army played a major role, and to Azerbaijan war heroes. Banners of the Azerbaijan divisions, weapons, and other mementoes of the war period can also be seen.

The display devoted to the republic's development in the 1970-80s—the establishment of new industries, or record crops of cotton, grapes, vegetables as well as achievements in science and technology, in the health service, education, and the arts. A map showing Azerbaijan's exports is also on view. There is a room containing items of the present-day folk arts and crafts—carpets, embroidery, carving, etc.

The theme of the exhibition in the last room is "Friendship and Cooperation". Colour slides, photographs, documents show Azerbaijan's wide international links and its contribution to the consolidation of the USSR. You can see gifts donated to Azerbaijan by its sister republics, by foreign countries and public figures.

The "Golden Treasury" room (admission by special permit only) contains unique collections of jewellery, arms, carpets and embroidery, the most valuable exhibits from the museum's archaeological, ethnographic and numismatic departments (the latter's collection consists of 100,000 exhibits and is second only to that of the Hermitage).

Round the city tour continued. Back in Ulitsa Shaumiana, do not miss the plaque on No. 16, where one of the pioneers of the Soviet oil industry Gulballa Aliev (1879-1971), Hero of Socialist Labour, lived. A famous repairman of oil installations, he had the gift of "seeing oil underground".

His former apprentices now work in Azerbaijan as well as in Siberia, the Urals and abroad.

Petrovskaya Ploshchad *(Petrovskaya Square)*. In the past this was a dusty down-at-heel place with a lot of quays. It was here that the detachment led by the 26 Commissars camped before their last tragic journey. A **monument to** one of them, **Grigory Petrov**, is a reminder of the fact.

Before Government House was built, the square was used for parades, mass rallies, etc. The four-storey building to be seen today in the centre of the square was specially constructed to accommodate the **Lenin Museum** (architect G. Medjidov, 1960), a branch of the Central Lenin Museum in Moscow.

Seven thousand exhibits in the museum tell the story of Lenin's life and work, of the Communists' struggle for the triumph of the revolution, for the construction of socialism and communism in the country, as well as of the revolutionary movement in Azerbaijan and of Lenin's links with it. Lenin attributed great importance to Baku as the leading industrial centre in the Caucasus and, after the establishment of Soviet power, as an outpost of socialism in the East. Lenin never visited Baku, but, as Kirov said, "...though far from the black oil derricks, he had a clear vision of Baku and its proletariat as a stronghold of the Revolution, and from the earliest days of his all-embracing leadership he always remembered Baku's workers. Lenin felt the distant beat of Baku's heart..."

There are also documents on the history and present-day activities of the Azerbaijan Communist Party, an integral part of the CPSU.

The neo-classical building behind the museum, once an apartment house (architect von der Nonne, 1883), is the **Baku Maritime School**.

We end the tour by walking along Ulitsa Shaumiana. On the left is the Youzhnaya Hotel, further on, on the right—the **Committee of People's Control** of the republic.

> People's Control is a form of socialist democracy. It is via the People's Control groups that the working masses exercise control over the economy, culture and bring influence to bear on government decisions.

Thousands of Baku's citizens elected to these groups at general meetings of their collectives monitor the fulfilment of state plans by the plants, offices, etc., at which they work, investigate breaches of discipline, bureaucratic delays, with the aim of improving management, work organization, etc.

Just before the Azerbaijan Hotel is the Dynamo Stadium. This popular sports club was set up in the 1920s by physical culture enthusiasts. For several decades (from the 1930s) the Dynamo arena was Baku's sporting centre. The club has produced ten world champions and world cup winners. It has a wrestling school with some great names to its credit, for instance the Dadashev brothers, one of whom now heads the republican wrestling team. The famous composer and conductor Niyazi, the holder of Azerbaijan's weight-lifting title for ten years, began his sporting career with the club...

Having completed our round tour of the city we are now back at the Azerbaijan Hotel. For tourists with only one day to spend in Baku we suggest the following variation to the last part of the route: get off the trolley-bus at Maiden Tower to see part of the Old City *(Icheri-Shekher)*. Cross the road, climb up to Maiden Tower and have a look at the historical monuments near it. Then turn right and walk to Shemakha Gate.

Leaving the fortress, Ploshchad Nizami *(Nizami Square)* opposite, turn right again and, having completed a circle, return through Ulitsa Djaparidze to Prospekt Neftyanikov. The rest of the route—as above.

As this prolongs the tour you might like to have lunch at one of the restaurants, the Bukhara or Multani, in the old buildings near Maiden Tower.

We suggest that tourists with several days at their disposal, however, follow the order of excursions set out in our guide.

FROM THE OLD CITY TO THE SEAFRONT

Route: Shemakha Gate—Bukhara and Multani Restaurants—Maiden Tower (Gyz Galassy)—Djuma Mosque—State Museum of Carpets and Folk Crafts—Palace of the Shirvan-Shahs—Revolution Garden—Health Zone—Seafront—"Baku's Venice"—Baku Bay—Pearl and Sahil Restaurants—Passenger Seaport.

Walking tour. Time: about 2.5 hours.

To reach Ploshchad Molodyozhi *(Youth Square)*, the starting point of the tour, take trolley-bus 3 to Dom Pechati *(Press-House)*, or go by metro to Baky Soveti Station. Either way, the old fortress walls will be on your right; within them is the historical centre of Baku, *Icheri-Shekher*, i.e. "inner city" as opposed to the "outer city"—*Bayir-Shekher*—outside the fortress.

We choose to enter the Old City via **Shemakha Gate** because opening onto the busy Shemakha road it used to be the main gate of the city. For about a thousand years a lively stream of traffic—peasants driving bull-carts, brilliant cavalcades of horsemen, camel caravans, and occasional pilgrims—poured across the drawbridge over the moat (since filled in) and through the arch with its massive iron-cased double gates.

The drawbridge and gates no longer exist. Over the gateway there is a coat of arms: a bull's head (probably a symbol of strong defences) between two lions. To the right and left of the bull's threatening horns are the sun and moon (probably meaning "guarded day and night"). The image of the bull which has also been found on other structures and implements dug up by archaeologists may possibly have formed part of some ancient custom or cult.

The fortress wall still standing was the inner one. There was an outer wall about 40 feet off it. If the enemy succeeded in scaling the first wall they found themselves in a stone trap where they could be shot at by archers from all

View of the *Icheri-Shekher* (Old City) fortress wall as seen from Revolution Garden.

Baku's coat of arms in *Icheri-Shekher*.

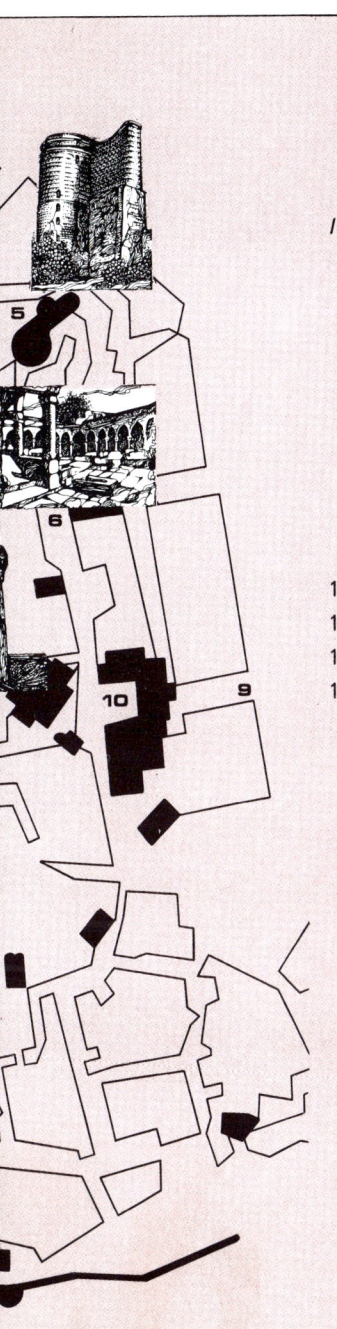

ICHERI-SHEKHER (OLD CITY)

1. Shemakha Gate
2. Bakihanov House
3. Multani Restaurant
4. Bukhara Restaurant
5. Maiden Tower *(Gyz Galassy)*
6. Market Place
7. Hadji Haib Bath-house
8. Djuma Mosque
9. Salian Gate
10. Gassym-beck Bath-house
11. Synyk-Kala Minaret
12. Shirvan-Shahs' Palace
13. Djebkhana Tower

sides. Between the walls was water-filled moat. The outer wall was pulled down when intensive building started in the 19th century.

In the course of the many wars over the centuries the walls were repeatedly destroyed and rebuilt. The present perimeter of the fortress emerged in the 13th–15th centuries replacing an older one. A stone found in the ruins of one of the walls bears the following kufic inscription, "Fortress built by the order of Shirvan-Shah Abdul Hidja Manuchehr II of the Kesranid line (1120-49)." On both sides of the gateway there are stones carved with texts from the Koran inserted into the walls. The walls have been restored several times.

The gate has another name—"Shah Abbas", under whom it was restored in the 17th century. In the 19th century, when a Russian garrison was stationed here, a second gate was installed next to the old one to provide for two-way traffic.

Now enter the citadel, *Icheri-Shekher*, a unique historical monument. This open-air museum of Azerbaijan culture has been in the main preserved. Luckily not one of the projects put forward at the beginning of the 19th century for a fundamental reconstruction of the Old City was carried out. Most of the important medieval structures—the caravanserais, the mosques, the baths, and of course, Maiden Tower and the Palace of the Shirvan-Shahs—are intact. The 14th–15th-century private dwellings, though, have nearly all been lost. In those far away times, the nobility and courtiers of all ranks lived at court, the clergy— round the mosques, the merchants and peasants bringing their produce to the market—in the caravanserais. The citizens, artisans and small-time traders, who were not very numerous, had fairly modest dwellings. It is hardly surprising, therefore, that none of the latter, apart from a few foundations, have been preserved.

Within Shemakha Gate there are two streets: one (to the

Old caravanserais in *Icheri-Shekher* have been turned into restaurants where the tourist can try the national cuisine.

right)—Malaya Krepostnaya Ulitsa *(Little Fortress Street)*—following along the walls, runs virtually all round the Old City; the other (straight ahead as you come through the gateway)—Bolshaya Krepostnaya Ulitsa *(Big Fortress Street)*—goes from Shemakha Gate to Salian Gate (directly opposite it across the city). This led out on to the southern, Iranian, road, running through the town of Salian. (Today Salian Gate opens on to Revolution Garden.) Bolshaya Krepostnaya Ulitsa, the oldest thoroughfare in the city, was lined with shops of all kinds. Some caravanserais were situated along it, and others closer to the sea which used to lap Maiden Tower. Two of them have been turned into restaurants.

A few yards down this street, on the right, is a modern building—the Azerbaijan Encyclopaedia Publishing House. Near the entrance is a **monument to Hassanbeck Zardabi** (sculptor E. Husseinova).

Zardabi (1842-1907) was a scientist, journalist, writer, educationalist and public figure. The first supporter of Darwin and the pioneer of natural selection in Azerbaijan, he was awarded a number of medals and diplomas for breeding new strains of plants. He is also known as the publisher of the first Azerbaijan newspaper—the *Ekinchi* (Ploughman), and as one of the founders of Azerbaijan theatre; he helped to set up the first girls' Moslem school in Baku.

Zardabi who worked unceasingly to introduce European culture to his people and to promote justice, is depicted, book in hand, leaning against a young tree bent in Baku's strong wind. The tree is shaped like a dragon which for the ancient Azerbaijanians symbolized good and later—evil. In the same way knowledge can be used for good or evil purposes.

Opposite the publishing house is the only part of the 18th-century Palace of the Baku Khans to have survived. The rest of this vast complex of chambers and outhouses was largely lost due to later rebuilding. Though bigger and better appointed than the Shirvan-Shah's Palace we will see at the end of the excursion, its architectural style is infinitely more simple.

The corner building, constructed at the late 19th century, dividing the street into two, houses the **Archaeological Centre** opened in 1983 to coincide with the world symposium on Eastern carpets which was held in Baku. Regular exhibitions of archaeological finds and ethnographic materials are held on the ground floor. It was in the same year that construction work was begun on the **House of Carpets** (architect R. Aliev), a permanent exhibition hall for displaying carpets made in Azerbaijan. To meet the growing demand for carpets all-Union and international auctions and fairs will be held here.

Gyz Galassy (Maiden Tower).

Turning into Bashennaya Ulitsa (Tower Street) there is a carpet shop on the left with large windows through which you can watch carpets being weaved. Here you can buy a carpet or a sample rug of your choice.

Further on you will find yourself in a narrow lane with a restaurant on either side. On the right is **Bukhara**, so called because it is set in a genuine 16th-century Bukhara caravanserai. It specializes in Azerbaijan national cuisine. Its 16 private rooms arranged round a patio are attractively decorated with low tables and benches and brightly-coloured *mutakka* cushions. The waiters wear national dress.

On the left is the **Multani** restaurant, also set in a 14th-century caravanserai where Indian merchants from Multani province used to put up. The Multani consists of two cellars with stylish interiors and period lamps over the tables. Above is a tea-room serving a choice of oriental sweets; it has nine private rooms, two of which are furnished in oriental style—with carpets and *mutakka* cushions. Note the 14th-century ventilation shafts in the wall as you enter the building.

Past the caravanserais is the famous *Gyz Galassy* **(Maiden Tower)**, a structure unparalleled for its architecture, whether in East or West. Rising to a height of 90 ft, it stands much as it did a thousand years ago, though today it is not the waves of the Caspian Sea, but the noises of a modern city that wash up against it—a few dozen yards away is busy Prospekt Neftyanikov (note some useful shops here selling records, books, etc. The Chinar foreign currency shop is also nearby). A source of endless legends the tower's name, age and purpose remain a mystery.

Erected on a coastal rock face which protected it from dampness and from tunnels being dug under its walls the cylinder-shaped Maiden Tower has a strange projection at its base which gives it the appearance of a retort. The projection is conventionally referred to as a buttress, but scholars tend to discount the view that it was built for defence purposes, or to give the tower additional structural strength, or to protect it from erosion by the sea waves. Nor has anything been found within the "buttress" to suggest that it served as an additional chamber or secret room. Another riddle is the masonry of the outer walls—smooth below it starts to be ribbed from about halfway up the tower and "buttress". Was this for decorative purposes, to break the monotony of the huge expanses of walls, or is the different style of stonework accounted for by different building periods. Experts favour the latter view; it is even thought there may have been more than two stages involved in the construction of the tower, a theory that is confirmed by the existence of two more projections adjoining the "buttress". Note an arched opening fairly high up the tower walls markedly different from the rest of the narrow, look-out slits. In size and shape it resembles a door or gateway. This is borne out by the fact that the floor of the chamber within has been worn away, as if by the constant passage of feet. There is also a well-preserved slot, presumably for a doorbolt. But if this was a door, how could it have been reached at such a height? The fragments of cantilevers embedded in the wall just below the opening suggest the presence of a staircase or drawbridge.

We know when the upper part of the tower was finally finished—a plaque set in the wall high above the ground tells us that this is: "The Tower of Massud ibn Daud." The fact that the inscription is in kufic script dates it to the 11th–12th centuries. The inconspicuous position of the plaque, as well as the absence of epithets, titles, dates, etc., indicate that the inscription refers to the builder of the tower, rather than to the shah in whose reign it was constructed. The builder's name, moreover, is known (his son put up the round tower in Mardakyany—an Apsheron village). The archaic shape of Maiden Tower, the change of masonry style, and colour of the stone darker than that of the earliest of the dated monuments of the Old City—the 11th-century Synyk-Kala Minaret—suggest that it can be attributed to an earlier date of around 5th–6th centuries. The ruins of the obviously ancient buildings around the tower support this suggestion.

Here are some legends giving various interpretations of the tower's name. Once when Baku was under siege by an Arab host, and its fall seemed inevitable, the custodian of the sacred flame worked a miracle: he raised a great fire over the tower which took the shape of a maid with a sword in her hand. One version of the legend goes that the enemy gave up the siege in fear, another says that the Fire Maid appeared in the enemy camp at night and slayed the Arab commander.

The following interpretation of the name may be the most plausible: Maiden Tower means Virgin Tower or one never taken by the enemy. There are other defence structures elsewhere in Azerbaijan bearing the same name.

Walking round the tower (the best way to do this is to descend to Prospekt Neftyanikov) you will notice that the top has been reconstructed. Evidently built originally for religious purposes, the tower also served as a look-out post and as a stronghold where people could shelter in time of an attack. As the danger of conquest increased the

tower's defence value grew—it was built higher and fortified. It may have had machicolations. A historical source states that the top of the tower was damaged by catapults when under seige by the Mongols.

Now let's go inside. A narrow spiral staircase leads up to a landing about 90 ft above ground level. This is a good place to appreciate the tower's strength: its walls are 16 ft thick at the base and 13 ft thick towards the top. Its eight floors could accommodate over two hundred men. Lighting was provided via narrow windows. The purpose of the clay pipe running down the whole length of the walls is unclear—it may have been a sewage system, or used to channel gas to a sacred flame on top of the tower... From the landing one gets a magnificent view of Baku bay and the Old City. Mind the steep steps as you descend.

We will now proceed to view the cluster of old buildings round Maiden Tower that came to light as a result of recent clearance work in the Old City (buildings of no archi-

17th-century market place in *Icheri-Shekher*.

An exhibition of stone-carving is now to be seen in the market place.

tectural value were pulled down following the removal of the majority of the inhabitants of the fortress to Baku's new residential areas). These historical monuments bear witness to the fact that in the early Middle Ages the tower occupied a central place in the social life of the Old City.

In the 15th century a new nucleus was formed round the recently built Shirvan-Shahs' Palace, but following the fall of the Shirvan-Shahs in the 17th century and with the construction of the Baku Khans' Palace near Shemakha Gate, the town centre shifted back to the area round the tower where it was to remain up to the beginning of the 19th century when Baku finally emerged from its fortress shell. On leaving Maiden Tower walk down the steps to the well-preserved 17th-century **market** with its large inner courtyard, bounded by the *iwan*, a columned arcade of pointed arches. Note the similar arcade at the Shirvan-Shahs' Palace which we will come to later on in our tour. The use of independently standing columns, hitherto considered rare in view of the seismic conditions characteristic of the area, is of particular interest to experts. Displayed in the marketplace is an exhibition of stone-carving. Among the exhibits are 13th–18th century tombstones and sarcophagi from the cemeteries of Baku and Apsheron; carved stones with inscriptions and figures of people and beasts from the sub-

Another view of the market place and its exhibits.

Entrance to the Djuma Mosque, today the Museum of Carpets and Folk Crafts.

merged Sabayil fortress brought up from the bottom of Baku bay; medieval tombstones carved in pre-Islamic style (pre 7th century); and finally stone figures of rams and horses symbolizing wealth, valour and courage (17th–19th centuries). The fine-grained Apsheron lime-stone combined with the skill of the Azerbaijan stone-masons results in wonderful works of art. There is a similar collection in the Shirvan-Shahs' Palace.

The following monuments next to the market are of interest: the **Hadji Haib bath-house** (15th century); the **Lezghi Mosque** (12th century), and the old foundations under the **Djuma Mosque** (early 20th century). The Sunday services were held in the Djuma (Friday) Mosque (Friday is a holiday for the Moslems).

Note how much lower is the market place compared to the level of the modern street. This gives one an idea of how much higher Maiden Tower would have appeared in the 17th century.

Have a look at the weather-beaten stone with an intricate inscription set in the walls at the entrance to the Lezghi Mosque. It comes from an earlier building. It was customary in the Moslem world to insert such stones (from earlier structures), which were highly valued in view of their exquisite calligraphic stone-carving and the fact that they were often inscribed with texts from the Koran, in buildings of a later date. New mosques were traditionally built on the foundations of old ones, and their decoration often imitated that of the earlier buildings. Inscribed stones were sometimes brought from cemeteries to adorn a new structure. This was in full conformity with Moslem religious practice. For according to the Moslem faith the grave of a believer has to be levelled with the earth and, once this has happened, the tombstone with its sacred text can be used to further the divine purpose elsewhere.

The Djuma Mosque contains the **Museum of Carpets and Folk Crafts.** Carpets have been weaved in Azerbaijan from time immemorial. Apsheron, in particular, was famous for its wool and natural dyes: fig leaves were used to

19th-century carpet. 19th-century tapestry rug sack for bed linen.

obtain ochre, madder—for red, saffron—for orange, while the skin of pomegranates gave a beautiful brown-rusty colour... Travellers in the Middle Ages had high praise for local dying skills.

Azerbaijan carpets were mentioned by Abu Ajafar, Muhammad Taberi (9th–10th cent.), Marco Polo (13th cent.) and others. Carpets of characteristic Azerbaijan design are sometimes to be seen in the paintings of European artists—Hans Holbein ("The Ambassadors"), Jan van Eyck ("The Madonna with Canon van der Paele") and Pinturicchio ("Virgin Mary").

The exhibition opens with a display of carpets woven like tapestry which rivals that to be seen in Washington's famous Textile Museum. This is the earliest type of carpet and can be traced back to the Stone Age.

There are seven main types of Azerbaijan smooth-faced carpets: *palaz, jejim, kilim, zil', soumak, vierni* and *shedde*. Each has local variations. Local natural dyes are used and motifs reflect local flora and fauna. This room, with its as-

tounding variety of pattern and colour is the museum's pride.

Research done by the leading Azerbaijan crystallographer Khudu Mamedov has shown that carpet patterns often imitate crystal forms, for instance, of silica or mica. Another characteristic feature is the absence of depth in the design which achieves its impact by intricate interweaving and by the enigmatic juxtaposition of the various elements in the pattern. The Eastern weaver, unlike his European counterpart who leans towards realism, does not strive to imitate nature, but rather the inner structure of things.

On view are *palaz* carpets with their bright horizontal stripes, vertically striped *jejims*, multicoloured *kilims*, and exquisitely fine *viernis*. There are wall to wall carpets and smaller items: saddle bags *(khurdjuns)*, horse-cloths, covers, curtains, cases of all kinds—for jewellery, scissors, combs, etc.

Carpets had universal application, as is demonstrated by the model of Azerbaijan period interior arranged in the mu-

Saddle bag, late 19th century.

19th-century holster embroidered in gold thread.

seum: they were used for decoration and warmth, on walls and floors, to screen off recessed spaces. According to ancient custom, the dead were carried on carpets to their last resting-place. Thus carpets accompanied man throughout his life.

The other rooms contain a great variety of carpets with pile. The four main types of Azerbaijan pile carpets are classified on the basis of origin: Kubá-Shirvan, Ganja-Kazakh, Karabakh, and Tabriz. They differ in technique, design, and composition. Quality is judged by the density of weaving (the number of knots per square decimetre) and by the texture of the pile.

New carpets used to be spread out in the street for passers-by to walk over—it got even more compact that way. They were then washed, and trodden on again. A would-be purchaser would run his thumb along the edge of a carpet—to feel the density of wool, or count threads. The finished item was rolled up—if it unrolled of its own accord, the carpet was considered to be a good one.

The Kubá-Shirvan carpet (produced in Baku, among

Embroidered hat from the town of Nukha, late 19th century.

Decorated 19th-century copper pail.

other places) has a density of 1,600 knots per sq.dm, high quality wool with fine deep pile. Of this type, the *Heela-butah* variety is noteworthy with its colour scheme recalling the sea, sand and sky—characteristic features of the Apsheron landscape—and its usage of the pear-shaped *butah* pattern typical of the Azerbaijan (and Indian) decorative art. This pattern is reminiscent of a cypress tree or a flaming torch; indeed, some experts think it was a Zoroastrian symbol. Then there is the *Ghymil* variety, with its checkered design reminiscent of the local *shebeke* windows. The *Pirebedil'* and *Chichi* are tightly patterned carpets made in mountain villages.

The Ganja-Kazakh carpet has a density of 900 knots with coarse stout woolen pile. The pattern takes the form of large medallions and stylized flowers along the border. The colour scheme is bright red, white, black, ochre-yellow, grass-green. Bird or animal motifs are also typical. The *Ganja* (see centre of the display) is one of the most popular makes of carpet produced in this region.

Malaya Krepostnaya Ulitsa in *Icheri-Shekher.*

Inside the fortress.

The Karabakh has a density of 1,600 knots, and deep stout pile. Its distinguishing features are its high quality, large size, and the fact that it comes in sets of a similar pattern throughout. The so-called *dasty* consists of a main central carpet—*hali*, two narrow side ones—*kenare*, and the "head" carpet—*keleish*, or *bashlyk*. There are a total of 33 designs. The *Gasymushaghi* is noted for its outstanding juxtaposition of forms each with its own motif. The *Malybeili* consists of squares with snake-like geometric figures inside.

Tabriz carpets have a density of 3,600 knots per sq.dm, and are noted for their special technique as well as their artistic merits. Subject designs predominate. As most of them are produced in Tabriz in Southern (Iranian) Azerbaijan, they are known as Persian carpets.

Distichs *(beits)* by Nizami, Khayyam, Firdausi and other poets form a traditional part of the design. The most important lines of the verse are emphasized by being placed in medallions—*ketebe*. The carpet "Omar Khayyam with

His Beloved", is invariably admired both for its subject matter and for its quiet and subtle colour scheme.

Displayed together with the carpets are some splendid examples of craft works, together with items of domestic use.

There is a separate department of jewellery.

The gold pectoral from the Zivi hoard, as well as a mass of other items found in ancient burial mounds and tombs, testify to the high skills of the local gold-and-silver-smiths as early as the Bronze Age. Note particularly the wedding head-dress made of silver, and "mirror" belts—superb examples of the art of chasing, carving and embossing silver.

The last room contains objects of modern applied arts: works by well-known Azerbaijan artists, including the fa-

mous weaver Liatif Karimov. There are examples of modern jewellery, embroidery and articles made of metal and wood.

There are about 6,000 items in the museum's collection, over half of which are unique. Some of them have been shown at international exhibitions:

— a tapestry woven *Vierni* carpet, with a snake-like pattern that is thought to have symbolized a dragon (or water). *Vierni* means "dragon". Similar carpets are to be seen in the Victoria and Albert Museum in London. Due to exceptionally complicated technique they are no longer made;

— a *Pirebedil'* carpet dated the 1233 year of Hijra (1817–18), remarkable for its high density, intricate, beautifully balanced pattern and quiet colour scheme;

— a *Heela-butah* carpet (18th cent.) made in an Apsheron village. For all its laconic colour scheme this carpet has

View of Salian Gate. *Divan-hana.*

a wonderfully expressive design. This type of carpet first appeared in the 16th–17th centuries;

— a *Khyrdagul'-chichi* ("small flowers") carpet, remarkable for its symmetry, rhythm and the unity of its pattern;

— a *sherbet-gaby*—a 14th-century copper sacred vessel for sherbet, richly decorated, engraved with calligraphic inscriptions;

— an *aynaly-kiamar* ("mirror" belt)—a 19th-century woman's belt decorated with fine filigree work;

— a *bashlyck* (head-dress)—engraved and embossed with minute balls of silver filigree work (18th cent.). Such wedding head-dress are no longer produced since the technique is too complicated.

The tour round the historical centre of Baku continued. A little further on, is the large **Gassym-beck bathhouse** of a later date (17th–18th cent.) and very different externally from the Hadji Haib bath-house you have already seen. Next to it is the **Salian Gate**, much smaller

One of the 18th-century gravestones on view in the Shirvan-Shahs' Palace.

View of the richly decorated entrance to the Shirvan-Shahs' burial-vault.

than Shemakha Gate via which we entered the Old City. Turn right and climb the hill towards the Shirvan-Shahs' Palace. You are now walking along Malaya Krepostnaya Ulitsa built parallel to the fortress walls by the Russian garrison for defence purposes: the artificial earthen embankment gave the soldiers easier access to the walls. Narrow stone platforms attached to the walls were used to hoist the cannon into place. This southern side of the fortress was strongly guarded against invasion. The uneven spacing of the towers and battlements was dictated by defence purposes.

On our way to the palace you will pass some 19th-century private houses. You now walk up lanes so narrow that only donkies could have been ridden here. There is another bath-house, Aga Michael (18th cent.), still functioning, with a big chimney which looks amazingly like a rocket. Climb a bit higher, past the Djinn Mosque (15th–16th cent.) and you will find yourselves before the palace.

The Shirvan-Shahs' Palace Ensemble (15th–16th cent.) was built when the Shah's capital was moved from Shemakha to Baku. This was the most prominent architectural complex in the medieval city, when the latter's importance was at its height. Some of the buildings, forming part of the ensemble, far surpass the palace in splendour. Despite the fact that the ensemble was constructed at different times with no single plan, it gives the impression of a harmonious whole.

The Palace is a two-storey structure: the ground floor with its narrow window-slits accommodated service rooms, the upper floor—state rooms. The lay-out and external appearance of the building is modest. Among its 52 rooms the octagonal domed audience room with its plain portal on the outside is of special interest. Built in the 15th century by Halilullah I the palace remained intact a hundred years. After Baku was taken by Shah Ismail, the palace was abandoned, and the contents of its treasury removed. The exterior was restored in the Soviet period. Now the interior is being restored to its original 15th-century appearance. In 1964 the palace was declared a monument of historical and architectural interest. Once restoration work is completed the palace will accommodate Baku's History Museum.

Adjacent to the palace is the ***Divan-hana*** rotunda, crowned with a faceted cupola of pointed arches echoing a similar arcade of arches in the enclosed courtyard. The stone carving of the portal—with its carpet-like intricate ornamentation, medallions enclosing kufic inscriptions and niche with deep-cut pendants—is striking. It is not certain whether the stones were first carved and then lifted into place, or carved *in situ*, but either way the technical skill and artistry involved are remarkable. The rotunda is often considered to be one of the gems of medieval art of the Orient.

> Its purpose, though, is disputed. *Divan* is said to mean "court of law". One rather lurid story has it that during trials, which were watched by the public from galleries round the courtyard, after sentence was pronounced, the criminal's head would appear from out

of an opening in the stone floor to be immediately struck off, while the body was disposed of into the Caspian Sea through a system of canals. However, *divan* may also mean "office", "state institution", and the rotunda was most probably the internal revenue office into which taxes were paid. Debtors may have been punished here. The mysterious opening in the floor is thought to have been made later, in the 19th century. There was a curious popular belief that this place could cure a nursing mother of loss of milk— hence another interpretation for the name of the building—"milk well". The site may have had religious associations in the pre-Moslem period. The still preserved wells, an underground chamber and recesses in the rock, probably to catch the blood of sacrificial animals, support the idea.

Having examined the buildings round the upper courtyard, walk down the steep steps of a narrow passageway leading from the *Divan-hana* into the middle courtyard. On the left is the ground floor of the palace, straight ahead, next

Synyk-Kala Minaret (11th century).

door to the ruins of the Bei-Kubad Madrassah Mosque (14th cent. at the latest), is **"the Dervish's Mausoleum"—the tomb of Seid Yahia Bakuvi, a court astronomer**. This octagonal chamber has a pyramid-shaped, tent-like ceiling, a small pointed arch leads into the burial vault. Further on (left) is the only memorial of the Turkish occupation of Baku in the 16th century—the **Eastern Gate with portal** facing the street (you can examine the portal later after having completed the tour of the palace).

Walking towards the minaret of the palace mosque, you pass through a doorway onto the lower courtyard, a place of Moslem worship. Straight ahead is the **Shah's family tomb**—*tiurbe*, with a stone dome decorated with geometrical design. Its portal is almost as splendidly carved as that of the *Divan-hana*. Skilfully ciphered in the oval above is the architect's name—Muhammad Ali. An inscription over the doorway states the purpose of the building and its date (1435). Next to the tomb is a mosque with a tall minaret. The following inscription can be read under the *muezzin*'s round balcony: "Built by the order of the great Sultan Halilullah I. May Allah glorify the days of his reign. The year of Hijra 854" (1444). Enter the mosque; the central nave is covered with a cupola; next to it are service rooms and the women's prayer-chamber. The altar, *mihrab*, is by the southern wall facing Mecca.

Pass through the women's prayer-chamber out into the far end of the lower courtyard, where the **palace bath-house** is. Discovered in 1936, like all Oriental bath-houses, it is sunk into the ground for coolness in summer and warmth in winter. Light is admitted via openings in the cupola ceiling, the only part of the building above ground. Heating was partly by hot air passed through special ducts under the floor and by hot water running in clay pipes along the walls and out into the bath-house—both ingenious and economical. The palace water supply system—it can be seen outside the bath-house—is also rather original.

On your way back through the middle courtyard note the stone slabs carved with animals and kufic inscriptions: these come from a building now submerged under the waters of Baku bay known as *Bayil Ghesri*. The mason's name and the date have been deciphered on the slabs—632 year of Hijra (1234–35). Climb back to the upper courtyard.

The ensemble does not impress by its size (it covers a total area of less than a hectare) or by its bright colours— the use of coloured tiles is practically nil. Nor are there any striking external effects. Its impact is achieved by the way the buildings harmonize with the natural landscape: the way space is ordered; its compact unpretentious scale plus the imagination and skill which has gone into the architectural decoration. The play of light and shade emphasizes the stone carving, while the blue sky sets off the cupolas and minaret. The golden ochre colour of the old stone, the spaces between the columns and arches... All this taken together accounts for the charm of the palace.

The important role played by the interior decoration of the palace should be mentioned. Imagine precious carpets, hangings of silk and cloth embroidered in gold instead of the bare walls; *chirakh* lamps shimmering in the corners, the Shah's splendid throne; carved window frames, and other objects symbolizing the exquisite luxury of the Orient... Plans are now underway to restore the interior decoration of the ensemble.

On leaving the palace turn right and following its wall (built, it is thought, in the 19th century) approach the Eastern Gate (or Murad's Gate).

From the viewing platform near the gate there is a good view of the bay and the Old City with its maze of winding streets.

Beyond the bay, to the left, in clear weather the largest of Baku's new housing developments, Akhmedly, can be seen.

The Old City, a historical and architectural monument, is to be further excavated and restored. Some of the monuments are not easy to reach: for example, the two minarets which can be clearly seen from here over the flat roofs. The one to the left belongs to the Beiler Mosque, the other, to the right, is the Synyk-Kala Minaret. The earliest (11th century) of the dated monuments in the Old City, the latter building, having got its name (*synyk* means "damaged", "ruined") after being damaged in a siege, is distinguished by its solid, somewhat heavy archaic form. Once restoration work is complete, all places of interest in the Old City—those already known about (of which there are now over fifty), and those still to be excavated and restored—will be made accessible to the tourist.

Your tour of the Old City is drawing to a close. Having returned to the main entrance of the Shirvan-Shahs' Palace ensemble, go down the hill and turn right towards the fortress exit. On your way you pass the entrance to the *ovdan* (15th century), an underground water reservoir, which is reached by a vaulted staircase.

> The following legend attaches to the reservoir. A meek small man once lived in the Old City who spent his life helping people. In addition he took upon himself the task of cleaning the underground galleries of the reservoir. For that on certain days he would go up to the hilly part of Baku, climb down a well there and, after walking many miles underground up to his waist—and in some places up to his neck—in water he would emerge on the spot where you are now standing. He would take no money for his pains. Sinking and looking after wells was considered holy work in Azerbaijan. When the good man died, no one was found who could do the job as well as he had done, and the well containing the best water in the fortress—the local inhabitants called it *shirin* ("sweet") water—dried up.

Walk through the gates out of the fortress into Kommunisticheskaya Ulitsa *(Communist Street)* near the Baky Soveti Metro Station. Turn left and you will find yourself in **Revolution Garden**. This is a good place to sit down on a bench and have a rest.

Called at first Mikhailovsky, and then, after the governor's residence had been built just below it, Gubernatorsky (Governor's), this is the oldest public garden in Baku. It was laid out in the early 1830s.

Of course, 150 years ago the garden looked very different. Tchaikovsky who visited Baku in 1887 wrote as follows about his stay there: "The only disaster is the absence of greenery. Due to constant drought and the rocky soil even the authority-maintained Mikhailovsky Garden is a sorry picture of withered trees and yellow grass."

In 1920 Baku had 0.6 sq.m. of greenery per head of population, today it has 20 sq.m.

Continue your tour excursion. The steep garden paths descend towards the sea. On the left through the trees you can catch a glimpse of the fortress wall—in fact, you are walking round the fortress on the outside, but in a direction opposite to the one you took on the inside. Near a fountain by the walls, is a cafe selling ice-cream. Further down the hill at the end of the garden is an open-air *chaihana* (tea-house).

The area between the cafe and *chaihana* is known as the "health zone". It was set up 25 years ago by a specialist in spa treatment, Professor Hassanov. Treatment, which is aimed at preventing the human body from aging, takes the form of gymnastics, massage, walking, running, deep breathing exercises, rythmoplastics, sea trips, music therapy, flower-inhaling (the scents of some flowers are considered therapeutic) plus the eating of fruit—grapes, figs, mulberries, etc.—under medical supervision. No medicines are prescribed. The zone which is open to everyone, is especially popular with the elderly. The basic idea of the treatment at Baku's health zone, i.e., a combination of exercise plus attractive natural surroundings, has found followers in the USSR and abroad.

Before leaving Revolution Garden we recommend a visit to the *chaihana*. Unlike the Central Asian *chaihana* where hot meals are served, its Azerbaijan counterpart serves only tea, in pear-shaped glasses, *armuds*, which keep it warm. But a *chaihana* means much more than tea-drinking: it is a place to meet people, relax, and be sociable—an island of Oriental tradition in the midst of a modern world.

Cross Prospekt Neftyanikov to the seafront along which runs one of the longest and most beautiful of the boulevards in the country—Primorsky.

Be careful when crossing the avenue: drivers in Baku, as everywhere in the Caucasus, it must be admitted, are very temperamental and not too willing to give the right of way to pedestrians—even on zebra crossings.

The seafront was built in the 1860s. Earlier, as you know, the sea had come up to Maiden Tower. As the sea receded the shore was built over. The road (the present Prospekt Neftyanikov) running between the warehouses and other buildings was to play an increasingly important part in the life of the town and with the beginning of the oil boom it was transformed into a vital transport artery, linking the old oilfields in the west of the city (Bibi-Eibat) to the refineries in the east ("Black City"). To enlarge the road the fortress wall facing the sea was pulled down, its stones sold, and the proceeds used to build the seafront. The work was done by the architect Hadjibababeckov (also known as Gasym-beck) who played an active part in building the new city *(Bayir-Shekher)*. At first there was no greenery. It was only in 1909 that trees were planted along one of the seafronts which from that time on became known as the boulevard. It

Sailing boats in Baku bay.   View of the seafront.

was not as long or as wide as it is now. It was not until the Soviet period that the far end was landscaped.

Let's walk down the boulevard (also known as Primorsky Park) which begins at the Intourist Hotel. It is nearly three miles long and has a pier jutting 275 yards out into the sea.

Now we come to **"Baku's Venice"**: a system of canals spanned by light bridges. The total length of the canals is about a mile, their depth is 5 ft. Not far away is the chess club, in a building shaped like a sombrero hat: it was here that Garri Kasparov, the youngest ever world chess champion, started his career. Nearby is the Neftchi Yacht Club and a similar club for children. Yachting and rowing are popular, though the winds are often too strong in the bay for these sports.

Scattered throughout the park are tennis courts, running tracks, various sports grounds, ping-pong and billiard tables, etc., all attesting to Baku's love of sport. At about 7 a.m., the park is full of joggers, young and old.

This is a good moment to take a 45-minute trip round the bay in a launch. Hungry tourists can have a bite to eat at one of the two restaurants (Sahil and The Pearl), or at the many cafes, tea-houses, etc., which are dotted all along the boulevard.

As our launch heads for the open sea, bound for Nargin, one of the many islands lying off the Apsheron Peninsula, let's take an imaginary journey along the republic's southern coast.

The Lencoran plain in the extreme south of the republic, jammed between the sea and the Talysh Mountains, is the second subtropical zone in the USSR, after the Black Sea coast. Citrus fruit and acca (feijoa) are cultivated here and so is tea; though the output is smaller than in Georgia, Azerbaijan tea is also of high quality. Over the last ten years the extensive cultivation of early vegetables has started. They are despatched from Lencoran, which has earned for itself the reputation of "all-Union vegetable garden", to many regions of the USSR. The main cities on the plain are Lencoran, the former capital of a principality, and Astara, divided into two by a river along which runs the border with Iran. The Talysh Mountains are known for the longevity of their inhabitants: Shirali Muslimov, who set a record of long life, died at the age of 168 in the village of Lerik. The famous Gyzylagach nature reserve, extending over an area of 200,000 acres, is situated north of Lencoran: a shallow gulf separated from the sea by a sand bank; it is the habitat of rare plants, animals and birds— the pink flamingo, the lotus flower, etc. The so-called "iron-tree", whose wood is so strong that machine parts can be made out of it, also grows here.

Still further to the north is the mouth of the Kura, the biggest of Azerbaijan rivers, with its source in Turkey. Most of the 500-mile-long stretch of the river within the republic is navigable. Kura means "capricious"—for the river used to flood fields and villages, causing great damage. The construction of the Minghechaour power plant and reservoir, however, helped to regulate the Kura's flow, which now wends its way, quietly and majestically, through Azerbaijan to the Caspian. Near its mouth is the town of Neftechala producing iodine and bromide; also noteworthy is the village of Bank where black caviare is processed and packed. The Caspian is fabulously rich in fish, particularly sturgeon (80 per cent of world stock), from which comes the famous Caspian (or Russian) black caviare. But its oil comes first as is testified to by the great number of derricks on islands, sand banks and along the whole coast.

Your launch is now far enough off shore to see the whole bay—from Cape Shikhov (on the right) to Cape Sultan (on the left). Its horse-shoe shape and the islands at its entrance make it into a well-protected harbour. As the launch turns, a lighthouse over one hundred years old on Nargin Island comes into sight. From here in clear weather there is an excellent view of Baku port, first in the USSR in terms of its oil freight and one of the largest in terms of its freight turnover. Most of the tankers and dry-cargo vessels putting in here have a keel shallow enough to sail up the Volga. The White Sea-Baltic and Volga-Don canals connect the Caspian to the White, Baltic, Azov, and Black seas. Bigger ships, and giant sea oil platforms, cranes, and oil rigs are also to be seen in the port. A ferry service—the first in the USSR—runs from here to Krasnovodsk, a city 200 miles away on the east coast of the Caspian.

As you near the shore you can enjoy the splendid panorama of Baku from the sea.

Having landed, continue your tour of the seafront, walking in the direction of the parachute-jumps tower (no longer in use), which carries an electronic display board indicating time of day, windspeed, temperature of air and water. Note the original design of The Pearl restaurant and the Children's Theatre (architect V. Shulgin). On your way you can watch TV in the open air, or weigh yourself (5-kopeck charge) on the numerous scales, or test your strength on a dynamometer. They say in Baku that the tasty national food requires one to keep a constant check that one's strength keeps pace with one's weight. There is a pavilion for special exhibitions, and a "Nature Conservation" pavilion where displays of Azerbaijan flora and fauna are arranged. As there is a luna-park on the seafront, you will be sure to find many children around. This is also a favourite spot among older people, who enjoy playing chess and nards here.

We now come to the Passenger Seaport (architects D. Akhundov, V. Shulgin, I. Orlova-Stroganova, 1970), a modern steel, concrete and glass building with two façades—one looking at the sea and the other—the city. It has a restaurant with both covered and open-air dining rooms. With seasonal adjustments (the Volga and North Caspian are frozen in winter) there is lively passenger traffic from the port. Every day at 10 a.m. the m/v *Sabit Orudjev* (named after an oil-industry pioneer) takes a shift out to the Oil Rocks platform.

Here the boulevard ends in the industrial "Black City"—with its oil refineries. The general development plan for Baku envisages the closure of the majority of these old refineries, or their removal to other parts of the city and extending of the boulevard to the housing district beyond. It will then have a total length of about 8 miles.

We have completed our present tour. We suggest that you take another stroll along the boulevard in the evening (it's near your hotel) when you will see it in a new guise— full of people and blazing with lights reflected in the waters of the bay. An evening walk along the boulevard is a good way of ensuring a good night's sleep.

MODERN BAKU

Route: Mustafayev Museum of Fine Arts—Magomayev Philharmonic Society—Baku City Council—Nariman Narimanov's Memorial Flat—the Palace of Weddings—National Manuscript Fund—Presidium of the Academy of Sciences—Press-House—Political Education Centre—Nizami Literary Museum—Bookshop Arcade—Samed Vurgun Russian Drama Theatre—Nizami Cinema—Akhundov Opera and Ballet Theatre—Biul-Biul's Memorial Flat—Akhundov State Public Library.

Walking tour. Time: from 2.5 to 3 hours. The starting point is the Philharmonic Society in Kommunisticheskaya Ulitsa, reached by metro (Baky Soveti Station) or trolleybus 3 (get off a stop earlier than you did on the previous tour).

We have toured Baku's medieval centre—the citadel. We would now like to take you round the modern city which, due to an excellent piece of town planning, appears to have developed naturally out of the old town retaining a lot of its national colour, while at the same time being a 100 percent European in appearance. New Baku was built astonishingly quickly: the oil-boom nouveau-riche industrialists vied with each other in erecting enormous mansions and public houses designed by Moscow, Petersburg and foreign architects. Despite the general European trend local building traditions manifested themselves: the high cost of land near the fortress walls made it sensible to build apartment houses with galleried patios—as per local prototypes except on a larger scale. The architect often fell under the spell of the monuments in the Old City imitating their elaborate decor and his predecessors' skilful use of landscape.

A good example is the corner house on Kommunisticheskaya (formerly Nikolaevskaya) Ulitsa, from where we start our tour. This five-storey building, belonging to the Sadykhov brothers, was built with a feeling for climate and local style: white, with loggias, balconies and a balustrade along the roof, it is crowned by a tower with arches and merlons round the top (architect G. Termikelov, 1912). Now look across the street at the second house from the corner—two-storey, elegant, reserved, with a portico in front and loggias at the side, built in the neo-classical style. It is the Mustafayev Museum of Fine Arts (our next port-of-call). Note the difference between the two buildings: the first is a happy attempt at stylization, later to be incorporated in local 20th-century architecture; the second could have been built in any European city. As is the case with all big cities, particularly where East and West meet, Baku has not avoided eclecticism. Still, as you walk round the streets, keep a look out for those attempts, often successful, to work out a modern national style. Note the imaginative forms of the glassed-in balconies (Baku's traditional *shushebend*), often overhung with creeping plants, the attractive local building stone, often finely carved—and you will see that modern Baku is a city not without a character of its own.

Now, you cross Chkalov Street (one of the most beautiful in Baku, named after the famous aviator who in 1937 made a non-stop flight to America over the North Pole), and make your way to the **Mustafayev State Museum of Fine Arts**. The museum occupies a mansion (we looked at it from the other side of the street), which belonged to one of Baku's rich men, Debour. It was built in 1888 by the architect von der Nonne. In 1920–22 it housed the Azerbaijan Revolutionary Committee. The Committee's chairman, Nariman Narimanov, lived and worked here.

The Fine Arts Museum was set up in 1936 on the basis of the arts department of the local history museum, and is named after Rustam Mustafayev, an artist who worked for the theatre. The museum's fund of over 10,000 exhibits was formed out of gifts from the central art galleries of Moscow and Leningrad and from private collections. The exposition is organised in chronological order following the main periods of world art and also the development of Azerbaijan art (representational and applied).

We begin our survey from the first floor (the stairs are to the right straight after the entrance).

Room 1 (to the left of the hall).

Paintings of the Italian, Flemish, Dutch, Spanish, and French schools of the 17th-19th centuries: "Sleeping Endymion" by Guercino, "At the Surgeon's" by Brouwer, "Smokers in a Tavern" by Ostade, "Landscape with Houses" by Molenaer; several French canvases, among them a landscape by Dughet.

Room 2.

West European porcelain, 18th-19th centuries: Delft, Wedgewood, Meissen and Sevres china.

Rooms 3-6.

Russian painting of the second half of the 18th to the beginning of the 20th century.

"Pilgrim" by Tropinin, "Portrait of an Unknown Lady" by Zhodeiko, landscapes by Shishkin, Kuindzhi. Some excellent early-20th century pieces: "Portrait of V. O. Girshman" by Korovin, Grabar's "Blue Pattern", a still life by A. Kuprin.

Rooms 7-9.

Soviet Art: painting, graphic works, sculpture, and china of the early post-revolutionary period. The rest of the first floor is devoted to Azerbaijan painting and applied art, pre-revolutionary and Soviet.

Room 10.

Azerbaijan ancient and medieval art: fragments of rock-carving from Kobustan; ceramic vessels of 2,000 B.C.; tomb stones with animal bas-reliefs of the 14th and 16th centuries, ornamental copper dishes from the village of Laghich (17th–19th centuries); copies of wall paintings from the Sheki Khans' Palace (18th century).

Room 11.
Works by Azerbaijan artists of the 19th to the beginning of the 20th century (Mirza Kadym, Navvab, Alibeck Husseinzade), which combine the classical Azerbaijan miniature form with elements of European realism.

Room 12.
Azerbaijan realistic painting of the late 19th-early 20th centuries. Landscapes, portraits and still lifes by Behruz Kengherli (1892–1922), the first Azerbaijan artist to be educated in Europe; the "A Hundred Types from Pre-revolutionary Baku" series and "Scenes of Old Life" by Azim Azimzade (1880–1943), a pioneer of graphic art in Azerbaijan, whose works are known for their sharp social criticism.

The room also contains jewellery, examples of national dress, embroidery, and 19th-century metal work.

Room 13–14.
Soviet Azerbaijan painting, 1920–30s. Carpets and other crafts.

The tour is continued on the ground floor (downstairs, turn left).

The display shows how contemporary Azerbaijan art has developed into one of the leading schools of Soviet multinational art.

Room 1.
Works by Michael Abdullayev, People's Artist of the USSR, known for his monumental paintings, include: the triptych "On the Fields of Azerbaijan", devoted to the Great Patriotic War of 1941–45, a series of works on India.

Room 2.
Works by Sattar Bahlul-zade, "the bard of Azerbaijan nature". The landscapes on display, among them "Azerbaijan Legend", "Kiapaz's Tears", depict a world both real and faerie.

Room 3.
Portraits of outstanding figures of Azerbaijan history and culture (by different artists).

Rooms 4–6.
Graphic art. The delicate, decorative, richly-coloured works on display represent a development of the classical illumination technique. Among them note particularly Maral Rahmanzade's work and the "Old Baku" series by A. Rzakuliyev.

Rooms 7–10.
These rooms are devoted to the generation of artists who began working at the end of the 1950s. Each with an individual manner of their own, they are united by love of experiment. Of particular interest are the works by Togrul Narimanbeckov of mixed Azerbaijan and French parentage, who was educated in Lithuania, and worked in Samarkand. His paintings (note particularly, "Mugam" and "In the Gardens of Geokchai") and murals, works for cinema and theatre display the vivid imagination and bright colours typical of Azerbaijan folk art.

Room 11.
Works by Tayir Salakhov, People's Artist of the USSR,

Azim Azimzade "The Family".

State Prize Winner, a leading Soviet artist. His "Repairmen" and "Morning Train" have won wide recognition, while his portrait of poet Rasul Rzah reveals yet another facet of his talent. Salakhov's works can be seen in the Tretyakov Gallery in Moscow and in private collections in the USSR, Spain, France and Japan.

On leaving the museum walk a few yards up to the beginning of Ulitsa Chkalova (*Chkalov Street*). On the right you will pass the Baku Communist Party Committee headquarters housed in a former grammar school (architect M. Botov, 1885), similar in style to the museum.

Turn left, towards the garden, and you will find yourself in front of the **Yuri Gagarin Palace of Young Pioneers**. Over 5,000 children take part in the activities of its 50 clubs, engaging in artistic, technical and other creative pursuits. The palace is particularly proud of its *Djudjalarim* (Chicken) children's song and dance group—named after a popular song which during its 30 years of existence has

Tair Salakhov "Nardaran".

won a lot of prizes and gold and silver medals at various contests and festivals.

Next to the Pioneer Palace is the **Institute of Eye Therapy**. In the unhealthy urban conditions prevailing in Old Baku trachoma and other eye complaints were common, therefore, the institute was one of the first medical establishments to be set up under Soviet power. The improvement in urban life has helped to eliminate these diseases. Today the institute specializes in delicate eye surgery.

Crossing the street we return to the spot from where we began our tour—the top of Kommunisticheskaya Ulitsa. This part of the town was long occupied by warehouses, oil-barrel makers' workshops, a market-place, there was even a circus in а wooden building. It lay between the Moslem cemetery and the city rubbish-dump. Strolling players would perform here, it was also the site of weekly bazaars. Eventually the city authorities decided to turn the area into a new city centre. First building to go up was the girls'

"*Khanaga* (bath-house) in the village of Pirshagi", 19th century.

Moslem school in 1901. Our first objective in the street is the **Philharmonic Society** building, formerly the summer club of the Public Assembly.

Its construction in 1912 (architect G. Termikelov) in the middle of Gubernatorsky (now Revolution) Garden caused a public outcry as several hundred trees had to be cut down.

The domed building with its elegant towers in renaissance style (later to be rebuilt in art nouveau style) brings to mind a mosque and minarets. Harmonising well with the surrounding greenery, it used to be the haunt of Baku's beau mond.

Concerts were given in the hall which has fine acoustics. Since 1936 it has been used by the Philharmonic Society.

The hall has seen performances by Chaliapin, Prokofiev, Shostakovich, Khachaturian and other great musicians. The first performance of works by Uzeir Hadjibeckov and Muslim Magomayev, whose name the Society bears, have taken place here. The Society has a fine symphony orchestra led by conductor and composer Niyazi, a choir, a song and dance ensemble, and a chamber orchestra led by Nazym Rzayev. It has a winter concert hall, seating 686 and an open-air one, seating 1,288.

At the end of Ulitsa Chkalova is the Sovetskaya Hotel and the headquarters of the Central Committee of the Communist Party of Azerbaijan (architect T. Abdullayev, 1983). The administrative building a little further on (architects S. Dadashev and M. Usseinov, 1930s) is occupied by the Republic's Council of Ministers and the Central Committee of the Young Communist League (Komsomol). In front of it there is a garden on a slope with a cascade of waterfalls. In an old building in Kommunisticheskaya Ulitsa (next to the Sadykhov's mansion we have already talked about) the Party Committee runs an open Marxist University. Thousands of people study philosophy, sociology, history and economics at the University which has departments in a number of cities.

Further along the street you will recognize Revolution Garden and the Baky Soveti Metro Station. The modern station building provides an interesting contrast to the fortress wall behind it. The seven-storey building, a former apartment house (arch. V. Sarkissov, 1912–17) opposite accommodates several state organizations, among them the Baku Institute for Housing and Town Planning. It is worth crossing the street by the subway to peep into the courtyard of this house. Before doing that, however, walk up to the building straight ahead of you, with a tall tower and a clock on it. This is the **Baku City Council**. The foundations of this massive building built in renaissance style for the city council were laid in 1900. The authorities spared no expense on the project (the glazed bricks for the façade, for instance, were imported)—which was meant to show that Baku was, as Gorky put it, a city, "sitting on top of a gold

View of Ulitsa Chkalova and the Philharmonic Society building.

mine". Note the plaque on the wall to commemorate that Gorky once spoke here. The city council building was the swan song of I. Gosslavski, an outstanding architect known as "the Rastrelli of the Caucasus".

The best view of this building, however, is to be had from the other side of the road at the corner of Ulitsa Buniata Sardarova (*Buniat Sardarov Street*), named after a Party leader and statesman. It is now time to cross Kommunisticheskaya Ulitsa via the subway. Facing along Ulitsa Buniata Sardarova, you will see in the distance the colossal **monument to Nariman Narimanov**, the prominent Azerbaijan revolutionary leader. Seen from below it looks as if the flat-roofed houses of the Nagornyi district form a "pedestal" for the statue. In the past the district was inhabited by the poor whose interests were ardently championed by Narimanov.

Nariman Narimanov was born in 1870 in Georgia into a poor Azerbaijan family. Thanks to his ability

Baku City Council.

and thirst for knowledge he succeeded in acquiring a higher education. As a medical student in Odessa he joined the revolutionary movement. He started practising medicine in Baku and soon made a name for himself as a political writer. A follower and associate of Lenin, he dedicated his life to revolutionary propaganda among the Moslem population of Baku, Astrakhan and other places. Lenin praised Narimanov's work as a model of flexibility for the way he took account of the characteristics and psychology of the local population. Having been instrumental in bringing about the triumph of Soviet power in Azerbaijan, Narimanov headed the Revolutionary Committee and then the Council of People's Commissars, later becoming a co-chairman of the USSR Central Executive Committee. He died an untimely death in 1925 and is buried among the prominent Soviet statesmen in Red Square in Moscow.

View of the house where Nariman Narimanov, a prominent figure in the Revolution, lived. His flat is now a museum.

Not far from here, is No. 15, Kommunisticheskaya Ulitsa where Narimanov lived (1913–18). His flat is now a **memorial museum**. Here his consulting-rooms have been re-created as well as part of the study he used during the time he was the Chairman of the Revolutionary Committee. Authentic documents, personal effects, etc., telling the story of his life and work are on view. The museum always has a lot of visitors.

Before resuming our walk down Kommunisticheskaya Ulitsa this is a good moment to have a look at some places of interst just off it. In a green square, walking a block up Ulitsa Buniata Sardarova in the direction of the Narimanov monument, is a bronze **statue of Mirza Fatali Akhundov** (sculptor P. Sabsai).

M. F. Akhundov, playwright and philosopher, was as important for Azerbaijan literature as Pushkin was for Russian literature. The founder of Azerbaijan modern drama and narrative prose, the materialist philoso-

pher, educationalist and democrat, Akhundov was born in 1812 in Sheki. He studied in Ganja and was later a civil servant in the viceroy's office in Tbilisi. Living in the administrative centre and meeting progressive Russian writers and public figures widened his horizon. He began writing under the pen-name Sabuhki ("man of the dawn"), and devoted his life to overcoming the religious fanaticism and backwardness of his people. He promoted schools, books, a new phonetic alphabet, and progress in general. He was buried in Tbilisi where his house was turned into a memorial museum. There is another Akhundov museum in the town of Sheki, his birthplace.

Before you leave the square look at the corner building, where Ulitsa Sardarova meets Ulitsa Lermontova, a typical 19th-century apartment house with glassed-in balconies (arch. G. Termikelov).

Now go two blocks down Ulitsa A. Karayeva (named af-

View of the square at the intersection of Ulitsa Lermontova and Ulitsa Buniata Sardarova.

Palace of Weddings.

ter a Party leader of the 1920-30s) running parallel to Kommunisticheskaya Ulitsa to the **Palace of Weddings** in Ulitsa Polukhina (*Poloukhin Street*), often referred to as "the Palace of Happiness". This house was built for the millionaire Mukhtarov in neo-Gothic style by the architect I. Ploshko in 1911-12. In 1922-37 it was given over to a women's club named after A. Bairamov, a revolutionary murdered by the agents of the Mussavat government. The club was run by Bairamov's widow and played an important part in women's liberation. Though the Shariat law for women was never as harsh in Azerbaijan as in some other Moslem countries, a solitary life and the wearing of a veil not being universally practised, women (particularly as mothers) enjoying respect, yet a woman's life was nevertheless mainly confined to the home. Soviet power brought freedom to women. Today 45 per cent of the total labour force, 70 per cent of the teachers, 80 per cent of the doctors in Baku are women. Women account for 48,6 per cent of the City Council and play an important part in public life.

Opposite the Palace of Weddings behind a mosaic panel on the theme of "Music and Nature" is the Biul-Biul Music School. A little further on is the Urological Hospital, where kidney transplants and some other advanced methods of treatment are carried out. Ulitsa Polukhina (named after one of the 26 Commissars) has two more interesting buildings, both dating to 1899: the first in neo-Gothic style, designed by K. Skurievich, was formerly the Caspian-Black Sea Co. head office, today it is the Public Prosecutor's Office; the second was built by E. Skibinski as a private house. In national romantic style, and by far the smaller of the two buildings, it has fine stone carving reminiscent of those of the Shirvan-Shahs' Palace. It is occupied by the **Architects' Union**.

One block beyond the Architects' Union is the Taza-Pir Mosque, the largest in Baku and the centre of the Moslem religion in the Caucasus. Two blocks to the left of the mosque, in Ulitsa Ostrovskogo (*Ostrovsky Street*), is a **museum of Djalil Mamedkulizade** (1866–1932), a dramatist and short-story writer.

Mamedkulizade was born in the ancient city of Nakhichevan. He worked for a time as a teacher, and later started publishing a popular satirical journal, *Mollah Nasreddin*, at first in Tbilisi and then in Baku.

Now return to the Palace of Weddings, and continue along Ulitsa Polukhina till you reach Kommunisticheskaya Ulitsa. Across the road is the **Buniatzade Institute of National Economy**. The building, a former high school, was designed by D. Buinov, 1901-04. The institute, one of the youngest in Baku, has 6 departments (teaching 11 main subjects—planning, the economics of labour and trade, statistics, book-keeping, etc.), and research centres, including a centre for the economic and social development of Baku. The latter centre is working on a long-term plan for the city.

Taza-Pir Mosque.

Next comes the first stone building in the street—formerly the girls' Moslem school (architect I. Gosslavski, 1898–1901), now the **Manuscript Fund of the Academy of Sciences**. The fund has the best collection in the USSR of the Near and Middle East 9th–19th-centuries manuscripts: nearly 45,000, in Azerbaijani, Arabic, Pharsi, and Turkic. It also has a collection of early printed books and of 19th-century periodicals. Here too are kept the personal archives of prominent men of Azerbaijan culture (19th–20th centuries).

A permanent exhibition is arranged in three attractive rooms on the first floor: Room One contains unique examples of 9th-19th centuries manuscripts; Room Two—medieval miniatures; Room Three—examples of applied art and calligraphic writing. The following exhibits are of par-

18th-century miniature. Illustration to Nizami's poem *Layla and Majnun*.

ticular note: the original manuscripts of *Shah-nama* by Firdausi, *Bustan* and *Gulistan* by Saadi, works by the poets Hafiz and Djami, of Nasreddin Tussi's unique astronomical table, of Avicenna's *Canon of Medicine* and others.

There are grounds to suppose that prior to the Arab invasion there were a lot of books in Azerbaijan—for writing in various forms had been known since earliest times: viz., the pictographic writing found in Kobustan and numerous inscriptions on buildings, tombs, jewellery and household objects. Indeed if the production of books had not been highly developed in the pre-Islamic period, the medieval manuscript with its fine calligraphic writing, gilding, binding and illumination would hardly have been pos-

19th-century papier-mâché folder.

sible. All the pre-Islamic books perished, however, at the hands of religious fanatics, or as a result of wars and invasions. The Arabic script in which the Koran was written was considered to be of divine origin, which explains the great respect attached to the art of calligraph in the Moslem world. It required a special talent and long practice. No other culture has ascribed to writing such aesthetic and even ethical importance—"pure writing" signified a "pure soul". The formal ban on depicting living beings, the human figure in particular, gave rise, on the one hand, to a flourishing decorative art; on the other hand, the ban was never completely obeyed—the folk art that had existed for thousands of years lived on in the art of miniature painting. An outstanding Azerbaijan miniaturist was Sultan Muhammad of Tabriz who left behind him a school of disciples and followers. His illuminations for Nizami's *Khamse*, Firdausi's *Shah-*

Detail of stucco-work from the building housing the Presidium of the Azerbaijan Academy of Sciences. Built by a Baku millionaire at the end of the last century and named "Ismailia" in memory of his son.

nama, Hafiz' *Divan* are among the world's great works of art. Some of these rare manuscripts are to be found in the museums and libraries of Baku, Moscow, Leningrad, Tashkent, Paris, London, Tabriz and Istanbul.

We now come to one of the best buildings in the town, the **Presidium of the Academy of Sciences**. It was originally built by one of Baku's millionaires to house a Moslem charitable society named "Ismailia" in memory of his dead son. Designed in Venetian Gothic style by I. Ploshko it was known as the Palazzo Ismailia. The fantasy of its stone carving, "an architectural symphony", delights the eye. It stands on an advantageous site with the 14th-century square fortress **tower Djebakhana** seen behind it.

The rest of Kommunisticheskaya Ulitsa to Ploshchad Molodyozhi was laid out in the 1940–50s. A printing-press and some other buildings of little value were pulled down revealing the fortress wall, which was restored. A terraced

garden was laid out along the wall. A fountain and stone steps join this new garden to an older one, named after the poet Sabir. A **monument to Sabir** is to be seen in the centre of the garden (sculptor D. Kariagdy, 1958).

> Sabir (1862–1911) was a major figure in Azerbaijan poetry. While remaining an essentially Oriental poet, he created a new, lighter, conversational, realistic, popular style devoid of the didactic tradition. He wrote satirical verse. Born in Shemakha, he lived in poverty and spent much of his life wandering. In his later years he taught oil workers' children in a village near Baku. "Sabir", meaning "patient", was his ironic pen-name.

We now continue our tour. The street leading directly on to Sabir Garden is the oldest in the city outside the fortress. This part of the busy Shemakha road was called Bazaar Street. In the past it was full of shops, taverns, stalls selling all manner of things including fried tripe (jyz-byz), barbers' and artisan workshops. Today the street looks quite different: named after G. Hadjiyev, a Party leader and statesman, it has been enlarged and built over.

Note the apartment block on the left at the top of the street, one of the first blocks of flats to be built in the So-

Press-House built in constructivist style.

viet period. Designed in the neo-classical style by K. Senchikhin, and popularly known as the "Monolith", it was built of concrete, rather than of the stone more usual for Baku. From here you can get a good view of another concrete building on the other side of the street—the **Press House** (S. Pan, 1930s). Its architecture reflects the influence of Corbusier's constructivist style. The building is functional, well suited to the printing-press and publishing business. Its unusual shape is reminiscent of a ship's bow with several decks and the captain's bridge on top, or of a book with its spine turned towards you. L. Ilyin, the Soviet architect who helped to draw up the Second Master Plan for the city, noted when speaking of "Baku constructivism" that constructivism was probably less in conflict with the city's old architecture, with its flat roofs, cubic shapes and straight lines, than was the case elsewhere.

Behind the "Monolith" building is an old market in an arcade, behind the Press House—the Central Department Store.

We advise you to cross the street here to have another look at the Academy of Sciences and the tower behind it.

Walking through Sabir Garden down to Ploshchad Molodyozhi, note a marble plaque near the steps. It commemorates the First Congress of the Communist Party of Azerbaijan held in 1920 in the Workers' Club that used to be on this spot. The congress which was illegal, united all the local Bolshevik groups, and laid plans for the revolution. The club was later moved to a building opposite, closer to Shemakha Gate. Today it accommodates the **Kirov Political Education Centre**, set up in 1924. The centre organizes lectures and seminars on political and philosophical subjects, promotes an exchange of information on the introduction of new methods in industry, conducts sociological research, opinion polls, etc. Next to it is the Republican Trades Union Council, known popularly as Dvorets Truda (Labour Palace).

Walking away from the fortress gate you approach

Ploshchad Nizami. Here on its lower terrace is one of the most beautiful buildings in Baku—the Nizami Museum of Azerbaijan Literature, originally built as a hotel. One of the first buildings to be constructed outside the fortress walls, its façade is decorated with dark blue and turquoise majolica. In the pointed arches are statues of outstanding Azerbaijan writers of different periods: Fisuli, Vaghif, Mirza Fatali Akhundov, Natavan, Djalil Mamedkulizade, Djafar Djabarly. The sculptures give the building a pantheon-like appearance.

A memorial Nizami Museum was opened in the building in May 1945. In 1949 a 20 ft. bronze statue of Nizami was erected in front of it (sculptor F. Abdurrahmanov). As no contemporary portraits of the medieval Azerbaijan poets have come down to us, we have no idea what they really looked like. Nizami is usually thought of as he is depicted in the painting by Khalykov.

Nizami Ganjevi (1140–1202), the brilliant Azerbaijan poet and thinker, was born, lived all his life and was buried in the Azerbaijan town of Ganja (now Kirovabad). He wrote, as was traditional in his time, in the language of classical Persian literature. Declining all invitations to be a court poet, he retained an independence of mind and pen amazing for the Middle Ages. His contribution to literature can be compared to that of Homer, Firdausi, Dante or Shakespeare. He wrote a major cycle of five epic poems—*Khamse*—including *The Treasury of Secrets*, *Khusraw and Shirin*, *Layla and Majnun*, *Seven Beauties*, *Iskendar-nama*. He influenced literature in most Eastern Moslem countries, his poetry serving as a model till the end of the 18th century: there are countless imitations of his *Khamse*, and over a hundred imitations (*nazira*) of *Layla and Majnun* alone, written in Pharsi and Turkic. The original manuscripts of his works and of his *Divan* lyrical verse (some of the latter may have been written in Azerbaijani), have been lost. The earliest copies at our disposal date back to the 14th century. "Nizami", meaning "master of words", was the poet's nickname.

The memorial museum was later enlarged and transformed into the **Nizami Museum of Azerbaijan Literature** to include the history of Azerbaijan letters from the early Middle Ages to the present day. Its 23 rooms contain over 3,000 exhibits: unique illuminated manuscripts, superb examples of calligraphic art, rare editions, works of scholarship in many languages, photographs and films, autographs of famous writers. The exposition follows chronological order.

Going through the heavy carved museum doors you will see a bas-relief representing one of Nizami's characters, Farhad. Next to it is a sculptured figure of the poet himself. Go up the marble stairs, through the foyer, where regular exhibitions are held, to the first floor. Rooms 1–14 are devoted to the ancient times and Middle Ages; rooms 15–18 on the second floor are devoted to the 19th-early 20th centuries; rooms 19–23—to the Soviet period.

Among the most interesting exhibits are:

— a Tabriz carpet (early 19th century) depicting a scene that can be traced back to the ancient Zoroastrian myths;

— copies of the earliest (15th century) written records of the first major work in Azerbaijan literature—the *Kitabi Dede Korkut* epos, plus copies of the manuscripts which are kept at the Vatican and Dresden Museums;

— a 16th-century copy of Hagani's *Divan*;

— a unique 15th-century copy of Nizami's *Iskendarnama*; later copies of *Khamse* of high artistic value;

— illustrations to Nizami's poems by prominent Azerbaijan artists; copies of miniatures from the Hermitage collection;

— works of the decorative and applied arts depicting subjects from Nizami; a decorative plaque (enamel, silver, mother-of-pearl) made by a master craftsman Hadji Khalykov;

— an unusual register of Eastern poems based on subjects from Nizami;

— a 17th-century copy of *Divan* by Fizuli; a vase with Fizuli's portrait;

— a shirt covered with quotations from the Koran which belonged to Panah-Khan, the ruler of Karabakh;

— a 1837 issue of the *Moskovsky Nabludatel* (Moscow Observer) newspaper with a Russian translation of Akhundov's famous poem on Pushkin's death;

— a miniature chess set given by Alexander Dumas to the Azerbaijan poetess Natavan.

Having finished your tour of the museum you have to complete a circle by walking round the fortress—from Kommunisticheskaya Ulitsa to Prospekt Neftyanikov and the seafront. This district was built over in the 1880s during the oil boom and the sudden rise in importance of Baku port. It developed into a trade and business centre. The first building in the area was the two-storey caravanserai-

Statue of Nizami, the 12th-century Azerbaijan poet and thinker.

View of Ploshchad Nizami showing the statue of the poet and the Nizami Literary Museum.

type hotel, now the Nizami Museum. Then came two arcades in 1896, followed by a three-storey house opposite them with shops on the ground floor. At the fork of Ulitsa Djaparidze and Ulitsa Zevina (named after two of the 26 Commissars), near the museum, is one of the biggest cinemas in the city—the Azerbaijan. In front of it is the **monument to Natavan**, the Azerbaijan poetess (sculptor O. Eldarov, 1960).

This to date is the only monument to a woman in the East. It should be noted, however, that Natavan was by no means the only outstanding woman in Azerbaijan history. There were other women poets, for example Nizami's contemporary who also lived in Ganja—Mekhseti Ganjevi; there were women musicians, singers and women warriors who at a time of crisis assumed command of the armies defending besieged fortresses (Baku included).

Natavan (1830–1897) was granddaughter of the last Karabakh khan whose vizier was the poet Vaghif.

Born in Shusha, she was well educated. Her best-known *ghazals* (form of Oriental verse), simple and heartfelt, were dedicated to her dead son. Natavan, who was the hostess of a literary salon, *majlis*, in Shusha, was also a talented artist. Dumas-père met Natavan during his visit to Baku in 1858 and was later to remember her with great warmth as well as the piece of fine needlework she presented to him. Natavan had progressive views and promoted culture and enlightenment. She is also remembered for her charity work (she built a water supply in Shusha, etc.).

We now walk down Ulitsa Djaparidze (*Djaparidze Street*) which is closed to traffic and is a favourite promenade place in Baku.

Return to the Nizami Museum and walk on to a garden with original fountains, one of the oldest gardens in the city. On the left is the Araz cinema, behind the garden is an Armenian church.

Walking through the garden or circling round it to the right past the Nargiz cafe, we continue our tour of this very popular Baku district. There are some shops on the right, among them a souvenir shop. Crossing a busy street we enter an arcade of book shops with figures of nymphs above the entrance. Parallel to it on the opposite side of the street is another arcade of workshops—watch repairers, engravers, etc.

Leaving the arcade, turn right to **9th January Garden** named in memory of 9th January, 1905 when a peaceful workers' demonstration was massacred by the Tsar's army in Petersburg. The garden was formerly known as "Molokan" for it was originally a parking lot for cabs which were mostly driven by members of that religious sect. In the middle of the garden is a sculptured group of three female figures popularly known in Baku as "Faith, Hope, and Love". Near a large pool of water is an attractive open-air tea-house.

Opposite the garden is the **Aliev Arts College**. Aliev was a well-known actor. Founded in 1945 originally as a drama school, today the college has three departments with over a thousand students. It runs a student theatre, a variety orchestra, and folk instruments ensemble. It also has a photo-and-cinema lab. The college trains actors, directors, painters, designers, craftsmen, critics, etc.

Further down Ulitsa Djaparidze is the **Society of Friendship and Cultural Links with Foreign Countries**. Set up in 1930, it now has 25 sections in Baku and in the provinces, at various plants, factories, collective and state farms, educational and scientific establishments with a total membership of 500,000. The Society maintains links with 780 public organizations in 119 countries abroad. It organizes exchanges of delegations, tourist groups, exhibitions, theatre companies, etc., and holds Days of the Soviet Union abroad. Artistes from Baku have been applauded in London, Berlin, Ankara, Kabul—in 24 countries for a past few years. Baku annually receives thousands of foreign guests. The Society helps them to meet leading figures in science and the arts, as well as workers.

On the other side of 9th January Garden is the **Actors' Club**, opposite the **Vurgun Russian Drama Theatre** opened in 1920 as the first revolutionary theatre in the Caucasus. Ever since it was founded the company has concentrated on the production of modern Russian and Azerbaijan Soviet plays, though classics are also produced. The building was reconstructed in the 1960s, and concrete latticed frames were set in the windows in imitation of the traditional Azerbaijan *shebeke*.

Returning to the bookshop arcade walk down Ulitsa Djaparidze to the Veten (Motherland) cinema, where there are often film shows for children, especially during the school holidays. The cinema occupies a former arcade (1896). There used to be a casino here. Opposite are some early 20th-century apartment houses.

Passing the cinema keep going straight ahead to Ulitsa

Karganova (*Karganov Street*). Turn left to the **Meshadi Azizbekov flat-museum**. Azizbekov was one of the Baku Commune leaders. Turn right to reach another busy central thoroughfare, formerly Torgovaya (Trade) Street, now Ulitsa Nizami. It is a popular shopping centre for souvenirs, jewellery, eastern sweets. There are craft workshops, a fashion house, and a tea-house plus tea-shop where the traditional Azerbaijan tea-glasses (*armuds*) are on sale. Though the people of Baku give preference to tea, coffee is also available at the tea-house for those who prefer it, as well as sweets and soft drinks.

Most of the houses in this district have been built fairly recently. With their archways, crenelated turrets and shady loggias, the two apartment blocks at the crossing of Ulitsa Nizami and Ulitsa Sameda Vurguna represent a search for a national style adapted to modern requirements and the southern climate. The comfortable apartments are occupied by oil-industry workers and engineers. The rent accounts for 3-5 per cent of their monthly pay as everywhere else in the USSR.

A plaque on another house at the same crossing tells us that Lev Landau, an outstanding physicist, the winner of Lenin, Nobel and other prizes, lived there from 1908 to 1924. His father was an engineer at the oil installations in Balakhany near Baku where Lev Landau was born. Later the family moved to Baku and rented an apartment in the house you now see, while Lev studied at commercial school and then at University. Though the scientist was afterwards to live in Leningrad, Kharkov and Moscow, he always took pride in his Baku origins.

Walk down Ulitsa Nizami to a small garden where there is a **monument to Nasimi** (sculptors T. Mamedov, I. Zeinalov, 1978).

> Nasimi was a great 14th-century Azerbaijan poet. He was born in Shemakha and later lived in Baku which at the time was the centre of Hurufism, a secret heretical sect with a following among city artisans

angry at Tamerlane's oppression. The sect dissented from orthodox Islam, interpreting in their own way the mystic symbols of the Koran. Nasimi was one of the sect's leaders. Travelling through the Middle East, he was seized in Haleb (Syria) and executed by Moslem fanatics. He died a martyr's death being skinned alive. Nasimi was a brilliant lyrical poet and a philosopher. At a time when Arabic and Pharsi dominated all over the Orient, he was one of the first people to write in his native Azerbaijani. In the teeth of Islamic dogma Nasimi sang the praises of Man in his poetry which was extraordinarily daring for the time. Man's great talent and passion, he said, made him equal to God.

The garden stretches to the State Bank building (arch. G. Termikelov, 1901) with its main façade on Prospekt Kirova. Walk down the avenue a little way to the junction with Ulitsa Dvadtsat Vosmogo Aprelya (*28th April Street*),

House at the intersection of Ulitsa Nizami and Ulitsa Sameda Vurguna.

named after the day Soviet power triumphed in Azerbaijan. The first telephone cable line in Baku was laid along this street in 1886.

The two buildings standing on either side of the road at the top of Ulitsa Dvadtsat Vosmogo Aprelya—the Nizami cinema (the best in town) and (opposite) the Azerbaijan Telegraph Agency and the editorial office of *The Communist* newspaper (in Azerbaijani)—form a single architectural ensemble. Designed by S. Dadashev and M. Usseinov (1930s), they are symmetrically placed, their façades representing a variation on the classical theme. Steps lead up to small, colonnaded porticoes. The exterior of the cinema building, which is crowned by an elegant central tower and has a high relief panel forming part of its decor, is somewhat more "fancy" than its austere administrative "twin" across the street. The ensemble was to set the style for later building in the street.

Now cross Prospekt Kirova by the subway to the Tele-

graph Agency building and return to Ulitsa Nizami. A little way up, on the left, is the **Akhundov Opera and Ballet Theatre** (in the former Mayilovs theatre built in the art nouveau style by architect N. Bayev in 1901–11).

The theatre was set up in 1920, a month after the establishment of Soviet power in Baku, and continued to develop Azerbaijan operatic art, founded by Uzeir Hadjibeckov at the beginning of the century. G. Sarabski, Sh. Memedova and Biul-Biul were members of the company.

The latter's name, meaning "nightingale", was the nickname given by the Azerbaijan people to Murtuzy Meshadi Rzy ogly Mamedov, an outstanding singer. His unique, easily flowing, beautiful voice is preserved on many a gramophone records and is often to be heard in Baku homes. Mamedov began his career as a *hanendé* folk singer: he later went to study in Italy and mastered the European art of singing. He

Nizami Cinema.

View of the Azerbaijan Telegraph Agency building and the editorial offices of *The Communist* newspaper.

greatly contributed to the study of folk music, and was made People's Artist of the USSR. You can learn more about his life in the memorial museum in his apartment situated nearby.

While national opera was created in the pre-Soviet period, the first Azerbaijan ballet ("Maiden Tower" by Badalbeili) was not to see the light of day until 1940. Nevertheless there are now some good dancers in the ballet company which is well known in many countries. Alongside the classical Azerbaijan operas "Layla and Majnun" and "Ker-Ogly" by Hadjibeckov, "Nargiz" by Magomayev, "Sevil" by Amirov, the following national ballets can today also boast a place in Soviet music — "Seven Beauties" and "The Path of Thunder" by Kara Karayev (Lenin Prize winner), "A Thousand and One Nights" by Amirov (State Prize winner), and "The Legend of Love" by Melikov. The theatre has been awarded the Order of Lenin and the status of Academic. It performs operas in Azerbaijani and in Russian.

The theatre building has revolutionary and political associations: it was here that Soviet power was proclaimed in Azerbaijan and that the 1st Congress of the Peoples of the East was held in 1920. And not far away in the former Public Assembly building (now the Officers' Club) in Ulitsa

Scenes from "A Thousand and One Nights", a ballet performance given at the Akhundov Opera and Ballet Theatre.

Sameda Vurguna, the first session of the Baku Soviet of Workers', Soldiers' and Sailors' Deputies—the first organ of Soviet power in the Caucasus—took place in 1917.

Now return to Prospekt Kirova and walk a block along it to Ulitsa Hagani (*Hagani Street*). Biul-Biul used to live in the corner building across the road and his flat here has been turned into a museum. On the ground floor of the same building are the **Artists' Union** and an exhibition hall.

Turn into Ulitsa Hagani near the Palace of Culture named in honour of the 26 Baku Commissars, and walk to a neo-classical building with statues of oilmen along the top of it (sculptor S. Erzia, 1925). Formerly Miners' Union house, today it accommodates the **Composers' Union**.

The next big building in the street is the **Akhundov State Public Library** (designed by M. Usseinov in 1949, built in 1960). It is decorated by statues in niches of Pushkin, Gorky, Nizami, Hadjibeckov, Zardabi, Mendeleyev, Rustaveli, Vurgun and Abovian. The library contains several million publications in many languages. As Akhundov (after whom the library is named) once said, "The day will come when we will own books, when we will receive access to books read in Europe and the New World". Despite the ancient written tradition it was not till 1730 that the

first book was printed in Azerbaijani. This was one of the first books to be printed in the East where printing was introduced considerably later than in the West (it is interesting that lithography was the first form of printing to reach the East).

Akhundov's dream was to be realized. In the early days of Soviet power libraries were opened to the public at large. The collection of books for public libraries was organized on a massive scale in the city. A contemporary poster appealing for the donation of books reads: "Having thrown off their chains, the proletariat are striving for knowledge." Today Baku's public libraries have over 11 million books and journals.

The Akhundov Library faces the already familiar Ploshchad Dvadtsati Shesti Bakinskikh Komissarov (*26 Baku Commissars Square*). The main entrance has an imposing portico with three arches and broad steps leading up to it.

FROM THE CITY CENTRE TO THE FORMER SUBURBS

Route: Lenin Square—Government House—Central Book Shop—Sabunchinsky Railway Station—Azizbeckov Petrochemical Institute—Dvadtsat Vosmogo Aprelya and Nizami Metro Stations—"Liberation" Monument—Hadjibeckov House-Museum—Azizbeckov Azerbaijan Drama Theatre—Ganjlik Metro Station—Lenin Stadium—New Housing Development.
Combined metro and walking tour for 2-2.5 hours.

Starting from the centre of modern Baku the excursion embraces two former outlying areas—*Shemakhinka* and a

Government House in Ploshchad Lenina.

wasteland north of the stadium, now the place of massive housing development.

We start out in Ploshchad Lenina (*Lenin Square*) with its imposing Government House building. As late as 1850 the place was a moor abounding in game, where people went shooting. In the 1930s it was a large vacant lot with the oil-works beyond. When in the early years of Soviet power it was being debated where to establish a public centre for mass rallies and demonstrations, the choice fell on this spot, though there were doubts concerning the cost of developing such a large area and removing the old oil-works. The project, however, was carried out successfully, and the district is now due for further development: the remaining industries are to be removed, the seafront boulevard extended, and blocks of high-rise flats and other buildings put up.

Ploshchad Lenina is as large as Moscow's Red Square and Leningrad's Palace Square put together. A public

Azerbaijan Hotel in Ploshchad Lenina.

competition held in 1934 for the best design for **Government House** was won by the Moscow architects L. Rudnev and V. Munts. The construction was delayed by the war. Government House is a 12-storey building accommodating a number of ministries and government departments in its 1,000 rooms. The culminating feature of the building is a 37 ft. bronze statue of Lenin (sculptor D. Kariagdy). The high pedestal bears the Azerbaijan state coat of arms, while below the statue there are stands for guests of honour at parades and demonstrations. It is customary for Soviet and foreign delegations to lay wreaths at the foot of the monument; here the Young Pioneers and Komsomol (Young Communist League) enrolment ceremony takes place; here soldiers swear an oath of allegiance.

Two of the city's main arteries—Prospekt Lenina and Prospekt Neftyanikov—intersect at the square which serves as the nucleus of the sorrounding district. On the left of the square is the 17-storey Azerbaijan Hotel, facing it is the Apsheron Hotel. Behind Government House along Ulitsa Hadjibeckova there are three 10-storey and two 16-storey apartment blocks. On the ground floor of one of the 10-storey blocks is the **State Art Gallery**, where various exhibitions including autumn shows of works by young artists are organized. On the ground and first floors of the 16-storey building to the right is the central book shop—*Dom Knigi*, selling a wide selection of technical literature, fiction (the whole of the first floor), books in foreign languages, dictionaries, etc. Attached to the bookshop is a conference hall where meetings with readers and publishers are arranged. In the adjoining building is the Baky Department Store, one of the biggest shops in the city.

Ploshchad Lenina, though created over a long period of time by different architects, has emerged as a single, unified composition. The district is due to be extended east to meet up with the Akhmedly residential estate. The area north of Government House near the railway station is also under reconstruction.

Walk three blocks down Prospekt Lenina (*Lenin Avenue*), past the Aeroflot Office (on the left), and you will find yourself back on Ulitsa Dvadtsat Vosmogo Aprelya (*28th April Street*), part of which you saw on the previous tour. The older side of the street (to the left as seen from Prospekt Lenina) harmonizes well with the modern side (on the right). To have a closer look at the varied architecture of the turn of the century, turn left and walk a little way down Ulitsa Dvadtsat Vosmogo Aprelya; note the former Lutheran church, set back from the street, built in Gothic style (architect A. Eiler, 1895–97). It has good acoustics and is used today for chamber and organ concerts.

Now cross to the other side of the street where you will find a Children's Art Gallery. It has four rooms. Apart from a permanent exhibition, temporary displays are also arranged here—some of which come from other republics. Further on, walking back in the direction of Prospekt Lenina, opposite the 10-storey Baky Hotel (architect G. Medji-

dov, 1970), you will see an attractive garden. It was laid out by members of Young Communist League during the day of voluntary communal work held in memory of Lenin in 1924, the year of his death. Across the road is the Samed Vurgun Garden named after the poet whose statue can be seen at the garden's entrance (sculptor F. Abdurrahmanov, 1959).

Samed Vurgun was one of the first poets of the Soviet period — he carried on the tradition of Azerbaijan poetry in the new historical conditions. His pen-name "Vurgun" means "enamoured" — he dearly loved his country, its natural beauty, and its people. His poem "Azerbaijan" is widely known and has been translated into many languages.

The garden was laid out on the site of the former so-called *hefte* (soldiers') *bazaar* — a dusty lot near the railway station where recruits waiting to board their trains would buy odds and ends from local traders.

Beyond the garden you can see the large building of the

Sabunchinsky Railway Station. The USSR's first electric railway line ran from this station linking Baku to nearby oil townships, Sabunchi and Surakhany.

Statue of Djaffar Djabarly, the founder of Azerbaijan Soviet drama.

Azerbaijan Railway Administration (architects N. Yakovlev and A. Sarkissov, 1956) and, a little to the left, the railway station. Up the hill is the white semicircle of the Karabakh Hotel (architects V. Shulgin, E. Melkhisedekov, 1975). Walking in this direction you will reach Vokzalnaya Ploshchad (*Railway Station Square*).

Directly opposite you as you enter the square is the façade of the old station (designed by Bruni in 1880, reconstructed by P. Vassiliev). No longer functioning as a station, it has been given over to various services. A big new station stands at right angles to one side of the square. Go round it and you will see a third station, the former Sabunchinsky Station (architect N. Bayev, 1926), from which the first electric railway in the country linked Baku to the Sabunchi and Surakhany oil-fields, and later to all the Apsheron villages. Like Baku's first station, it is built in the national style with a minaret-like tower. In the middle of the square is a monument to Djaffar Djabarly (sculptor M. Mirkasymov).

> Djaffar Djabarly (1899–1934), a playwright who made theatrical history during the 1920–30s. His play *"Sevil"* about a liberated Azerbaijan woman was successfully produced in Baku, Kazan and Central Asian cities; at each performance hundreds of women threw off their black veils.

The classical building across and standing at right angles to the square—formerly a secondary technical school (architect I. Gosslavski, 1900)—is **the Azizbeckov Petrochemical Institute**. Some outstanding scientists have taught at the institute, which was set up in 1920, including Academician Kurchatov, a prominent nuclear physicist. Among its graduates are 70 Lenin and Republican State prize winners, prominent geologists and oil experts working in the USSR and abroad, well-known writers and film directors and cosmonaut Vitaly Zholobov. Apart from having the largest student body (almost 16,000 students) in Baku, the institute is one of the best equipped

(100 computers) institutions of higher education in the city; 31 subjects are taught at its 16 departments (9 of which specialize in engineering). It has 61 chairs, 22 specialized research laboratories, a first-class library, and its own printing-press and publishing house. It maintains links with foreign universities. Twelve patents have been taken out in different countries, including the USA, Japan, France, Spain, Italy, for the institute's achievements in the desalination of sea water. Important research has been done in the following fields: directional drilling, oil and gas exploration and extraction; automatic computer process control in oil and gas production and in the chemical and petrochemical industries.

The railway station square as well as Prospekt Lenina is well served by public transport. One of the first tramlines in the city used to pass through the square. (Today it has been transferred to a parallel street). Trams made their appearance in Baku only in Soviet times. The oil magnates were unable to agree along which street the first tramline should go. Each man wanted to enhance his prestige by having it pass in front of his own house. It's hard to say how much truth there is in the story. The fact remains, however, that at the beginning of the 20th century a horse-drawn tram-car was the only means of public transport in the city. The horse-drawn tram-car made its appearance in 1889, the electric tram—in 1924, the electric commuter train—in 1926, the bus—in 1932, the trolley-bus—in 1943, and the metro—in 1967.

Now it is time to look at the metro—we start off at **Dvadsat Vosmogo Aprelya (28th April) Station**, a round pavilion with a big "M" on top, between the Sabuchinsky and the new railway stations. At the entrance there is a colourful panel decorated with transport motifs—from the wheel to the rocket.

With a total length of 25 km and 16 stations, the Baku metro, the first in the Middle East and the second in Asia after Tokyo, connects the north-east housing districts and industrial areas to the city centre. Three more building stages are planned to bring the metro's total length up to 60 km and the number of stations to 27.

Take an escalator ride down to the platform. Its position next to the railway station, and not far from the airport and passenger seaport, has made the station into a major junction with trains going in three directions. To find out which direction a train is going in, watch the electric indicator board over the entrance to the tunnel. Turn left at the bottom of the escalator. Have a good look at the station—the walls and pillars are faced with marble, the vaulted ceiling is lit from below which makes it seem higher. The city stylized coat of arms is on the back wall.

Board a train, and get off at Nizami Station, designed by Usseinov in the national tradition, one of the best-decorated metro stations in the city. It has a mozaic portrait of Nizami (by M. Abdullayev).

The domed above-ground part of the station is built into

Block of flats.

Narimanov Metro Station.

a housing block. Straight ahead is an apartment house with ribbed balconies. In front of a big house at right angles to the station entrance is a statue on a high pedestal of a woman throwing off the hated veil. It is called **Liberation** (sculptor F. Abdurrahmanov).

Walking out of the metro turn right and go down Ulitsa Ismailova (*Ismailov Street*) to the intersection with Ulitsa Ketskhoveli (*Ketskhoveli Street*) (both streets are named after revolutionaries). On the side wall of a modest house to the right you can see a high relief portrait of Uzeir Hadjibeckov, the composer. It was in this house, now a **museum**, that the composer lived and wrote some of the best Azerbaijan music, including the opera "Ker-Ogly". His personal effects, his Italian violin, his piano, etc., can be seen in the rooms. There is his death mask and the casts of his hands. On the ground floor there is a film room and a chamber concert hall. Here on 18th September, the composer's birthday, the best pupils from children's music

schools play his music. In the film room visitors can see films of Hajibeckov's musical comedies—"Arshin Mal-Alan" and "This One If Not That", and documentaries in which he appears in person. The guided tour of the house is accompanied by Hadjibeckov's music, including extracts from his *mugam* opera "Layla and Majnun".

"Layla and Majnun" was the first opera in the East. The music was written mainly for the orchestra while the singing is improvised as part of the *hanendé* tradition.

> It is very difficult for the uninitiated to understand the *mugam* art of singing. To a layman who does not appreciate its "tones" it sounds plaintive and involved, the melody impossibly intricate. The "tones", of which there are seven, are not the equivalents of the European major and minor keys but are specifically developed musical structures. One *mugam*, plus the instrumental interludes, lasts an hour or two. It cannot be written down with the European system of notation—the intervals are quite different for the cadences of each *mugam* are varied. It is related to the Arab and Iranian *makam* and to the Indian *raga* now popular in the West. *Mugam* is always accompanied by lyrics, usually about love. Scholars define *mugam* as a combination of rigid canon and free improvisation—"individuality breaking through regimentation", reflecting Oriental psychology and philosophy. The Eastern man sees art as a means of discovering for himself a basically unchanging world. *Mugam* for this reason is listened to with concentrated attention. Historically the cult of *mugam* may have originated in the Zoroastrian ritual. Incidentally, the Arabic name for the fire-worshippers' cult is *makam*.

On leaving the museum have a look at the sculptured group of a folk musicians' trio (by L. Signal and E. Mamedov).

Go back along Ulitsa Ketskhoveli to the intersection with

Ulitsa Shihali Kurbanova, turn right and walk down the hill to one of the biggest squares in the city—Ploshchad Fizuli (*Fizuli Square*). To the right of the square is a shop Mugam selling musical instruments and gramophone records, including *mugam* music. In the middle of the square there is a **monument to Fizuli** (by sculptors O. Eldarov and T. Mamedov, 1963). The high pedestal of pink granite is engraved with reliefs on the "Layla and Majnun" theme.

Fizuli was a 16th-century Azerbaijan poet and thinker. He was born and bred in Iraq among the Azerbaijan community which was forcibly moved to the country during Tamerlane's wars. Though he knew several languages he wrote mainly in Azerbaijani. He lived at the time when the Safevid state ruled by Shah Ismail was at the height of its power. Shah Ismail also wrote poetry and cultivated the Azerbaijan language. Fizuli's poems, as well as his works on philosophy and astronomy, had a great impact in Azerbaijan. He was buried in Kerbel, near Baghdad.

In the past Ploshchad Fizuli was a market place where one could buy cheap goods brought to town by the local peasants. The rich merchants from Shemakha and abroad would drive their pack animals on to the fortress, where the caravanserais and best shops were. But here, at the intersection of the Shemakha-Kubá main road and the local Apsheron road, the peasants would camp with their carts, donkeys and oxen. There were a lot of stalls and small shops and a brisk trade went on. In 1903 the market was transferred uphill to the Shemakhínka district where, in modernized form, it remains to this day.

In the 1930s a five-storey apartment block was built in the square. It looked so big among the crowd of surrounding one-storey houses that the whole district acquired the name of *beshmertebe* or five-storey. The reconstruction of the square continued into the 1950s, and in 1961 the **Azizbeckov Azerbaijan Drama Theatre** was built in the middle of the square. It is designed by G. Alizade in the national style.

Though the development of drama in Azerbaijan has its roots in ancient folk performances and pageants, it did not like the other Moslem countries have a professional theatre. An actor, a clown, was an object of scorn; only *hanendé* singers enjoyed prestige, though this was not even extended to the musicians who played the musical accompaniment for them.

Professional theatre started in Azerbaijan with a production in Baku in 1873 of "Lencoran Khan's Vizier", based on the play by Akhundov. You saw some exhibits connected with the first steps of the national theatre in the Hajibeckov Museum. The actors had a tough time at first: they were stoned and spat upon and there were attempts on their lives. Arablinski, the greatest Azerbaijan actor, was murdered. The posters bore the following note: "enclosed boxes for Moslem ladies". Female roles had to be played by men, the first actresses appearing only in Soviet times.

Today the Azizbeckov Drama Theatre has an extensive repertoire: apart from national classics—Akhundov, Vizierov, Akhverdov, Mamedkulizade, it includes Russian and world classics, Shakespeare in particular, as well as modern Soviet plays. An important period of theatrical development came in the 1930s when plays by Djabarly, Djavid, Vurgun and Rahman were extremely successful.

Having looked at Ploshchad Fizuli, walk back to Nizami Metro Station along Ulitsa Shihali Kurbanova. On your way, beyond the five-story corner block, on the same side of the road is an office building accommodating some ministries and state departments, and one of the tallest buildings in Baku, the Construction Research Institute. To the right of it is a secondary school. We now get back on the underground again.

Our next stop is **Ganjlik** (Youth) near the Lenin Stadium. This station is also worth looking at: its white airy columns create a feeling of space. Faced with marble, their capitals resemble flowers just about to open. Lights are concealed inside. At the exit is a mosaic panel with sports motifs. To get to the stadium, turn right and walk along a subway.

The **Lenin Stadium**, designed by Consiarski, Isayev, and Sergeyev, was built in 1951 on the site of a sand quarry. Its terraces set on a hillside are open to the sea with the 55 ft high north stand protecting the pitch from the north wind. The stands are divided into 28 sectors and hold 45,000 spectators. The turf for the pitch was brought from Lencoran. In addition to the main arena there is a covered one. Still under construction are field and track grounds, tennis courts, additional football fields, other games' grounds, swimming pools with stands for 800 people.

To the right of the stadium entrance is the Kirov Physical Culture Institute, set up in 1930, the first of its kind in the Caucasus. It has produced world and Olympic tennis and handball champions, as well as champions and prize-winners in wrestling, cycling and other sports.

A short walk from the institute is the new Cardiological Centre.

If you turn left on leaving the stadium you will find a park with a children's railway which functions in summer. Just below it is the Zoo.

But our main objective in this district is the major new housing development opposite the stadium. Built during the 1960-70s, the development has a uniform architectural style. Its centre is Ploshchad Pobedy (*Victory Square*), in front of you, round which are the Ganjlik Hotel, a polyclinic and apartment blocks. Beyond and to the right of the square are apartments for thousands of people. There is a department store, food stores, various service shops, a restaurant, hospital and a big cinema seating 1,200. In future the district will be extended along the avenue to join up with the Montina suburb.

Here our tour of modern Baku ends and we return to the metro. Before getting off at **Dvadtsat Shest Bakinskikh Komissarov (*26 Baku Commissars*) Station** to go back to your hotel, you may wish to see some more metro stations. We advise you to have a look at Narimanov Station. The fluted aluminium columns of its platform produce such a bright effect that one tends to forget that one is underground. At the same time there are elements (viz, the column stalactite capitals) of traditional architecture.

Tours Outside Baku

KOBUSTAN

You are most likely to go to Kobustan on an Intourist guided bus tour. The brief information offered here is intended to supplement the guide's explanations.

The rock-carvings at Kobustan, a state-protected reserve situated 40 miles south of Baku, date back to the Stone Age. We drive to Kobustan along the old Salian highway which goes south towards Iran. On the way are many interesting sights.

Bayilov district which used to be populated by self-employed oil-workers, fishermen, peasants, was taken over by the Navy for officers' and seamen's quarters when Baku port grew in importance around the middle of the last century. Today it boasts some oil-wells and shipyards one of which we pass. The yards build, among other boats, vessels for cleaning harbours of oil-slicks and rubbish. Formerly the barges which brought water from the Kura river to Baku were repaired in the dry docks here. The water was pumped into tanks standing on the hill above what is now the Intourist Hotel.

About 270 yards off shore here in the bay are the submerged **ruins of Sabayil**. We saw some of the stones from these ruins in the Old City.

At the end of Bayil Cape some springs of water can be seen flowing into the sea. They are known as the "Spring of Forty Maids". Legend has it that once 40 maids were attacked when bathing by some ruffians. In fright they turned into springs—they have been shedding tears ever since.

In Ploshchad Krasina *(Krassin Square)*, named after the Party leader and statesman, is the Oil Workers' Palace of Culture. Designed by the Vesnin brothers in the early 1930s, it was one of the first clubs to be built in a working class suburb. The palace which bears Lenin's name has an exhibition illustrating the history of industry in the district.

Ilyich Bay. Below the road, to the left, is a forest of derricks on a low shore line, looking somewhat unreal, like stage props. It became clear at the end of the last century that the seabed here was rich in oil, though extraction was not to begin until Soviet times. The oilmen's work was made possible after the bay had been filled in with rocks and earth from a nearby hill—you can see it on the right, it seems as if its top has been cut off by a knife. The first oil-well was struck here in 1923. This marks the start of the tapping of the offshore oil deposits in the Caspian. It was a forerunner of the Oil Rocks settlement which was to make its appearance in the late 1940s.

Bibi-Eibat. We pass the derricks of Bibi-Eibat, Baku's oldest oil-field. According to legend Bibi-Eibat (Aunt Eibat) was the name of a servant of a female saint who was buried here. To the right of the road is the grave and **monument to Hanlar Safaraliev**, a revolutionary worker who was treacherously murdered in 1907 and whose funeral turned into a mass demonstration followed by a strike in

Cardiological sanatorium—one of Baku's new buildings.

View of Ilyich Bay. The first oil-well in the Caspian was struck here in 1923.

which thousands took part—a notable page in the revolutionary history of Baku.

The Shikhov Balneological Clinic. The Bayil oil has medicinal properties. Apsheron is also rich in curative mud and thermal springs good for rheumatism, arthritis, eczema, etc. The Shikhov Balneological Clinic (to the left of the road) specializes in this kind of therapy.

The Shikhov Beach is the closest to the city and very popular. The adjacent area has been turned into a large 250-acre park stretching uphill over a formerly bare slope. Honorary visitors to Baku are often requested to plant a tree in the park.

From here on, for the rest of the journey, a little way off shore, one can see what looks like metal poster-beds. These are the invention of local anglers, and enable them to fish away from the coast.

Despite the oil production and other industry in the area the sea is not polluted here—environmental protection

measures are strictly enforced by the state. The recent slight reduction in fish stocks (due to several factors including the receding sea level) has been checked.

Primorsk Township (to the left) is lived in by workers from the Karadag cement plant, and oilmen. There are large gas deposits here that supply gas to the other Caucasian republics. Despite its industrial enterprises, the township is a good example of successful conservation policy: it is green, the sea is clean and there is a good sandy beach. In fact Primorsk is a popular summer holiday spot, frequented by the citizens of Baku.

The two **mountains—Kyargyz and Shongar**—to the right (15 miles from Baku) got their names from birds of the vulture species which were considered sacred by the Azerbaijanians and Persians in Zoroastrian times. Whereas the Hindu cremated their dead by pouring melted butter over them, the Zoroastrian fire-worshippers left their dead on high exposed places for the vultures to devour.

You are now in the Kobustan area, which, in translation, means "ravine land". The spurs of the Great Caucasus Range descend to the sea here along the river Djeirankechmez (in translation—"where the djeiran (saiga deer) will not pass"). The soft clay soil led to the formation of numerous ravines. The local rock surface has the following remarkable qualities: it lends itself to carving, while at the same time being extraordinarily weather-resistant. These factors were to play a role in primitive man's choice of this site for his open-air "picture gallery".

The rock-carvings were first discovered in 1939 by the Azerbaijan archaeologist and ethnographer I. M. Djaffarzade. During the 25 years he spent exploring the area, the scholar found about 4,000 petroglyphs on 700 rock faces of the Beyukdash and Kichikdash ("Big Rock", "Small Rock") mountains. He took in rubbings and catalogued each of them. His work was continued by the archaeologist D. Rustamov who found another 2,000 petroglyphs. In 1966 Kobustan was declared to be a national reserve and put under the protection of the state.

Apart from the extremely interesting petroglyphs, caves

that were man's abode in the Stone Age can be seen. The area which at the time was rich in vegetation and animals and good for hunting in view of its natural traps—narrow passages, steep drops, etc.—attracted human habitation. Note the holes drilled through the rocks with stone implements: here trapped wounded animals were tied up as provision against famine or unsuccessful hunting. The animals were probably tended—the first step towards domestication.

The men in the petroglyphs wear loin-cloths and have powerful legs as befits hunters who run fast. The women have their breasts and hips emphasized as symbol of procreation; their arms are not shown, but they are armed with bows. There are representations of cult ceremonies and everyday life. There is a picture of a group dance, for instance, which is done in a circle with arms on each other's shoulders—forerunner of the *yalla* danced in Azerbaijan to this day. Linguistically *"yalla"* is cognate to *"yal"* which means "food". The "food dance" was presu-

Ancient Kobustan.

mably a magic rite done before hunting. It might also have served as good training for huntsmen—nimble synchronous movements are essential in collective chase. Note the stone "tambourine" which emits a booming sound when it is struck, it was probably used for accompaniment to the *yalla* dance. There is a picture of people in a dugout boat, also of sea-going bamboo boats.

There are pictures of bulls, wild Coolan donkeys, rock goats, deer, lions, gazelles, wild boars, snakes, lizards; of various symbols and signs, including the cross and swastica symbols for the sun in the East. Most petroglyphs show the sure hand af a master for they display an ingenious use of convention in depicting the human figure and keen powers of observation in depicting the animals in movement or repose. Some are masterpieces of daring and realism, others are done over older carvings.

In addition to the rock-carvings, the traces of early man's camps dating from the Mesolithic period are to be

Kobustan rock-carvings.

seen at Kobustan, and twenty burial mounds and graves, the most interesting being the Firuz burial (8,000 B.C.).

The bowl-shaped depressions carved out in the rock were probably used for collecting rainwater, the blood of sacrificed animals or for cooking. Until quite recently, mountain shepherds used these "bowls" for boiling milk by dropping heated stones into them. It is quite probable that the ancients had a similar use for the "bowls". One such stone is known as the "Kobustan kitchen". Another notable find is a stone with an inscription left behind by one of Alexander the Great's cohorts.

Kobustan may be seen as a unique source of knowledge on the period from the 10,000 B.C. to the Middle Ages covering the fields of history, culture, art and archaeology. To end your tour you may wish to call in at the museum which contains a collection of excavated objects: tools and shells of non-Caspian origin—evidence of links with the Mediterranean and the Indian Ocean areas; early ceramic

vessels of the 6,000 B.C.; stone beads and other objects from the Firuz burial mound in which eleven skeletons of the Mesolithic period were found. The most interesting exhibits are traces of black resin-like glue for mending broken vessels or making tools and a crucible indicating that the ancient inhabitants of Kobustan knew how to smelt metal.

The exhibition also contains rubbings of the most artistically perfect rock-carvings; a 200-year-old Kobustan carpet, some modern works of art influenced by Kobustan, etc.

APSHERON

Depending on time available, season, etc., Intourist offers a choice of several routes around Apsheron taking in the monuments of medieval architecture, the holiday resort zone with its first class beach, and various oil installations, thus enabling the visitor to trace the development of the oil industry. The sights described below are included in these tours in various combinations.

Moskovsky Prospekt *(Moscow Avenue)*, a wide, modern motorway, follows the old road which connected Baku to the Apsheron villages with their small houses and gardens where the city people lived in summer, and to the small hand-worked oil-fields. It was known as Balakhany from the name of a village literally meaning "an extension". As from the 1870s, in view of the oil boom the road grew enormously in importance. The traffic of peasants taking their produce to market, or of city families moving out to their vineyards was replaced by lorries and camels loaded with oil-barrels.

The "oil rush" and newly-built millionaires' villas in the village of Mardakyany raised the issue of building a better road. This was not done, however, until 1915 and then only over the Baku-Mardakyany stretch. One of the most urgent town-planning tasks, facing the new Soviet administration, was to build townships for the oil-workers. The best architects were involved in the project which required vast investment. The 1930s oilmen townships were regarded as model pieces of architecture at the time in the USSR. The road to Apsheron passes one of these settlements named after P. Montin (on the right) now engulfed by the city.

A large industrial district has grown up during the Soviet period around Moskovsky Prospekt. There are dozens of engineering and electrotechnical plants, light industry and food processing plants. To the left is the biggest air-conditioner plant in Europe. Both this plant and Azerelectrotherm next door to it are of architectural interest. For all the giant scale of their production their horizontal structures harmonize well with the landscape, neither dominating it nor polluting it with noise and smells. Visits to the air-conditioner plant, the Novobakinsky oil refinery and other factories can be arranged by the local Intourist office. The refinery is undergoing reconstruction within the general plan for the reconstruction of Baku's oil industry.

Once the road passes the Azizbeckov Metro Station, one of the last within the city limits, with a bus terminal next to it, a housing development and the Avrora Metro Station on the right, you have left Baku proper.

The **Apsheron Peninsula** juts 40 miles out into the Caspian. The Shakhov Bank at the far end of the peninsula has been turned into a nature reserve (with water fowl, Caspian seals, saiga deer). There are various explanations of the peninsula's name: it is said to derive from *ab*—water and *shoran*—salt, as there are many salt lakes on Apsheron or, perhaps, from the ancient Turkic tribe of the Apsherons. Besides its industry it is known for its milk cattle, vineyards and orchards of mulberry, almond and olive trees. The local state farm of subtropical crops has unique saffron plantations, the food processing plant produces olive oil. The Apsheron canal irrigates a significant part of the peninsula's sun-baked land.

Visits can be organized to the Nardaran carpet factory, to the Shuvelyan state nursery garden, the Mashtaga subtropical crops farm and to the **Dendropark**—the Academy of Sciences' botanical gardens (in Mardakyany). Founded in

1926 by the outstanding scientist N. Vavilov, who undertook to prove Azerbaijan's suitability for both drought-resistant and moisture-loving subtropical crops, it is known as "the garden of the five continents". Over one thousand five hundred species of plants from all over the globe grow over its 28 acres: exotic trees—*Carica papaya*, paper mulberry, *Liodendron* ("tulip tree") and *Arbutus* ("strawberry tree"), a large (over 40 species) collection of pomegranates, olive trees, etc. Henna and basma, still imported, are being acclimatised, as well as some medicinal herbs. Links are maintained with most botanical gardens of the world.

Near the entrance to the Dendropark is a high relief portrait of Sergei Yessenin, a Russian lyrical poet of the Soviet period. In the gardens itself there is a museum dedicated to the poet who wrote there his *Persian Themes* cycle inspired by Azerbaijan poetry and music and his *Ballad of the 26* about the Baku Commissars.

The northern shore of Apsheron is a green oasis and has long been a popular holiday resort zone. It has an uninterrupted stretch of lovely sandy beaches. In between its old villages with their orchards are sanatoria, holiday camps and pensions.

In summer the Bilghia pioneer camp for construction workers' children can be visited. This is a good place to bathe and have a rest.

Apsheron's medieval castles were built in three lines for defence purposes—along the north-east coast, the centre of the peninsula, and in the south near Baku. Maiden Tower and probably some other towers (now lost), were included in the latter line of defences. The castles stretch north to Beshbarmag Mountain and south to Kobustan. They are linked by some historians to the Roman expeditions which built forts and observation posts along the strategic Caspian coast. This is confirmed by local tradition: one of the oldest villages on the peninsula is called Ramana and this is where one of the biggest castles is, built, probably, on the site of an older fortress.

The **Ramana Castle** (mid-14th century), situated in the centre of Apsheron on a rocky hill, dominates the area.

This impressive structure is not unlike its West-European counterparts. The central tower, 45 ft. high, is surrounded by a wall. The defences are well-planned: the entrances are set in different directions to baffle the enemy. The towers and machicolations allow of cross-fire. The castle was virtually unassailable: the tower commanded the surrounding landscape. Besieging armies were subjected to a barrage of stones and flaming oil, which was in plentiful supply in the ancient oil fields all round the castle. These fields remain unchanged to this day and form an ideal backdrop for the fortress.

The **Mardakyany Castle** (14th century) towers over the flat roofs of the village round it named after the ancient tribe of the Mards. The village is particularly popular with the inhabitants of Baku who own or rent summer bungalows here. There are, in fact, two castles in Mardakyany: one with a round tower, the other, the bigger of the two, with a square tower. The latter castle is immediately visible as one approaches the village, though it is not built on a hill. Its layout is similar to the castle at Ramana: the central keep surrounded by a wall. The square tower, nearly 80 ft. high, of roughly hewn stone withstood cannon balls and battle rams. The corners are rounded by pillars which fulfilled both a supporting and decorative function. A winding staircase inside one of the pillars leads to all five floors of the tower. The stone steps begin a few yards off the ground—they were reached by a rope ladder which could be pulled in by the castle garrison.

The merlons and battlements round the top of the tower are impressive. The fortress wall also has rounded corners and smaller towers at intervals for the purposes of cross-fire. Within the walls there are over 30 jug-shaped receptacles hewn from the rock for storing grain, and a well. There is a magnificent view of the sea and of the old cemetery with its half ruined tombs from the top of the castle. Both the Mardakyany and Ramana castles were restored in the Soviet period.

Next to the castle is the Tuba-Shakha Mosque (1482–83) containing an exhibition devoted to the Apsheron castles. Among the exhibits are copies and translations of the text of

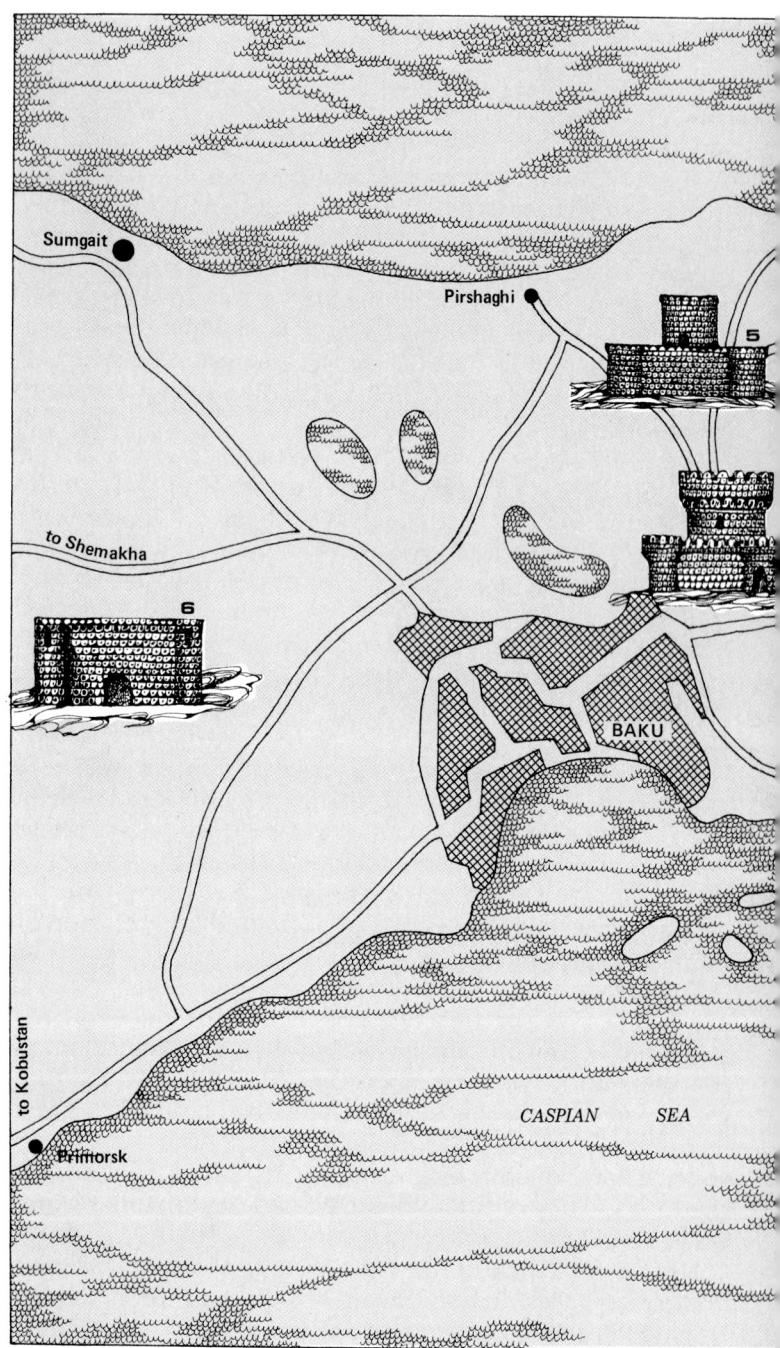

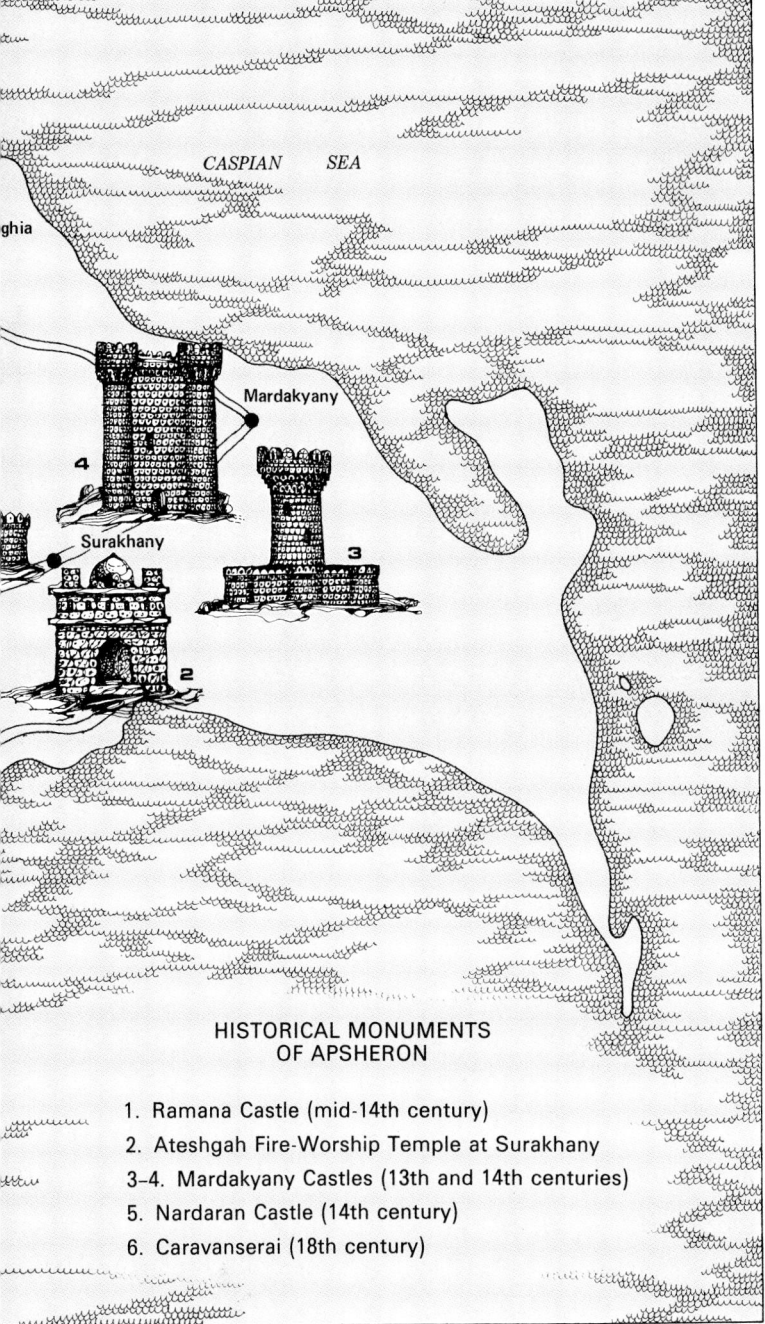

HISTORICAL MONUMENTS OF APSHERON

1. Ramana Castle (mid-14th century)
2. Ateshgah Fire-Worship Temple at Surakhany
3-4. Mardakyany Castles (13th and 14th centuries)
5. Nardaran Castle (14th century)
6. Caravanserai (18th century)

the inscriptions on two stones dating back to 1187. They were found at the gates of Mardakyany castle by the Russian ethnographer Khanykov in the middle of the last century and sent to the Petersburg Academy of Sciences. The original stones are in the Hermitage.

Ateshgah is an Indian—or to be more exact Parsee—temple built in the 17th–18th centuries near the natural vents of flaming gas in the centre of Surakhany, a town long famous for its "white oil." On the introduction of Islam to the region, all local Zoroastrian temples and altars were destroyed, so it may well be that the present temple stands on the site of a far older one. In the Middle Ages, when Azerbaijan's links with India were very close, the merchant caravans were followed by Parsee pilgrims flocking to the "sacred flames". That is the origin of this unusual structure: a strange mixture of local architectural traditions plus features of the ancient Indian fire temple. The pentagon-shaped building surrounded by a blind wall with

Round Tower of the 13th-century castle in the village of Mardakyany.

a guest-room *(balakhana)* over the gate (a traditional feature of Apsheron architecture) is similar to a medieval monastery fortress. Cells for pilgrims line the walls inside and surround the main altar in the centre of the temple—a square-shaped pavilion with an onion dome. Openings in the walls permitted a view of the eternal fire on the altar inside. There were other flames at the four corners of the altar roof—the gas being conducted up stone pipes. The earliest building in the temple is the stable—1713. Some of the inscriptions on the stones set in the walls are in Sanscrit. One of them mentions a merchant—Kanchanagar—who donated the central altar in 1816. Ateshgah was restored in 1969; an exhibition was arranged within the temple and the altar flames rekindled.

Oil Rocks has long been known for its oil and gas which seeped up from the sea bed to the surface. A few centuries back maps warned sailors against the "Black Rocks"—black because they were covered with oil. "At

14th-century castle in Mardakyany.

night-time there is a fine view of the city from the sea, it is not unlike Marseilles," wrote A. Ostrovsky, the Russian dramatist. "A burning rag was thrown overboard and the sea caught fire—such a phenomenon is not found anywhere else in the world." This all pointed to the existence of oil deposits under the sea here. They were not to be tapped however till 1920s. Today Oil Rocks is a town on the sea—it has 125 miles of streets (platforms) and a population of 4,000. Most of the inhabitants work in shifts—a week on the Oil Rocks, a week on shore. The people live in blocks of flats, attend evening school and a branch of Baku's Oil Industry Technical School; they eat bread from the local bakery and lemons and tangerines from the local hot-house; there is a lemonade plant on Oil Rocks and even rose-beds. There is a daily newspaper, a cinema, and a garden. Crime is unknown and drinking is not allowed. Oil Rocks is no place for bad mixers—all work, rest, studies, sport or recreation has to be collective. A team spirit is

Helicopter pad from which helicopters fly to Oil Rocks, a township built in the Caspian for deep-sea oilmen.

View of the "streets" in Oil Rocks, a town on the sea built on piers.

especially needed during the storms when the platforms shake under the onslaught of the sea. People go out in groups with their arms round each other's shoulders in order not to be washed or blown off the platforms. Work at Oil Rocks requires courage, endurance, professional competence, a sense of duty, and a sense of humour.

Each November a ceremony is held to remember the workers who lost their lives here during the storm of 1949, shortly after the first fountain was struck; flowers are thrown into the sea and a few minutes' silence is observed.

A visit to Oil Rocks takes a whole day: a four-hour trip by motor boat one way (more in stormy weather). Visitors who are pressed for time can visit Oil Rocks' "younger brother", the Serebrovsky Oil Installations (named after the first Azneft manager). It is similar in all respects, but on a smaller scale (11 miles of platforms), and can be

reached by bus over an artificial dam, and then a pier stretching several kilometres out to sea.

One gets a good view of the surrounding landscape from this dam. Note that the environment is not polluted—no smell of gas, no oil-slicks on the water; the wells (as is the case with the wells at Oil Rocks) are hermetically sealed. The 150-mile oil and gas pipelines, running either along the pier or along the bottom, allow to pump the condensed gas even from the far-off Bakhar deposit straight to the shore.

The **Sattar Bahlul-zade Museum**. A permanent exhibition of Sattar Bahlul-zade's (1909–1974) works is arranged in a beautiful mosque with two minarets (arch. Ziver-beck, 1908) in the centre of Amirajan, not far from the house where the artist was born and brought up. The poetic landscapes convey an image of Azerbaijan that is at one and the same time fairytale and recognisably real: Lake Gei-Gy-

View of the houses for oilmen belonging to the Serebrovsky Oil Installations.

oll, the Nakhichevan and Karabakh mountains, the Kubá gardens and the peculiar charm of Apsheron. Bahlulzade's canvases "Caspian Beauty", "The Ancient Flames of Surakhany", "Bilghia", "Buzovna" and others will help the visitor who may be put off by what appears to him to be an arid landscape enlivened only by oil derricks and pumps, to appreciate the peninsula's austere beauty, its brilliant colour contrasts: blue sky, green and blue sea, grey rocks, purple trees against a background of yellow sand... The artist is buried in the village cemetery. The grave-stone (sculptor O. Eldarov, 1980) is original: a full-size bronze statue of the artist holding a picture frame in his hand through which the surrounding landscape—lake, hills, trees—can be seen.

Razin Settlement. This settlement is named after Stepan Razin, the leader of the peasant war in Russia (1670-71). Razin camped with his followers in a cave on top of a nearby mountain here. The mountain became the venue for the first May Day revolutionary meetings. The present settlement was founded on 1 May, 1925. Today it is one of the largest and best-appointed Baku suburbs.

On your way back from one of the Apsheron tours, if you are not tired out, ask your bus driver to take you to *Sharg Bazary*, the new bazaar built in Eastern style behind the Sabunchinsky Railway Station (you can also reach it by trolley-bus 10). It has 14 brightly-coloured cupola of an Oriental palace. Inside are souvenir and jewellery shops, a kebab-shop, a tea-house decorated in national tradition, *tendir* ovens for baking traditional bread. A wide choice of fruit, flowers, herbs, etc., are on sale.

SUMGAIT—KHOUDAT—KUBÁ

This tour, like the Apsheron tour, takes you north, but along another road—the historical Shemakha highway. A short way from Baku the equally ancient merchant road to Kubá branches off the highway. Once these roads were travelled by camel caravans, their bells jingling, loaded with carpets, silk, grain and, on their way back from Baku, with oil, salt, fish. Today this motorway—Tbilisskoye Shosse—leads to the capital of Georgia—Tbilisi, from which it gets its modern name.

The first sight to be pointed out is the **11th Red Army Memorial** (sculptor T. Mamedov) in the centre of a circle of buildings. The memorial is conceived as a group of soldiers carrying the banner of the Revolution. The banner blown by the wind is reminiscent of a flaming torch. On the left—a clinic serving rural areas, where patients are treated by leading Baku specialists, and the Azerbaijan-Film Studios.

We now pass Alatava—"grey flat-stones": once a desert, today a massive housing development is being built here. The unusual concrete apartment block with honeycomb balconies near the road was constructed by the travelling mouldings method.

Entrance to *Sherg Bazary* (Eastern bazaar).

The **town of Hydralan** (meaning "retailer") was an old caravans' stop. Today it has some important industries: a pre-cast concrete plant, a furniture factory, a brewery, a battery-chicken factory. In the future this satellite-town will join up with Baku.

At the crossroads to Shemakha and Kubá, we take the right turn to Kubá.

On the left we pass the **Djeiranbatan Reservoir**. Though filled only during the spring floods it supplies water to the plants and factories in Baku and Sumgait, and irrigates Apsheron.

On the right we get a panoramic view of **SUMGAIT**, Azerbaijan's second industrial centre with a population of 200,000. This city boasts one of the biggest Soviet tube-rolling mills, a synthetic rubber plant based on natural gas, an aliminium and phosphate plant, the Sumgaitchemprom chemical plant. The industrial complex has been created since the 1950s. Previously the place was an arid steppe with a small village on the river which is dry for most of the year, thus its name—Sumgait (*su*—water, *gait*—come back). The city was founded in 1949, and was built by thousands of young volunteers from all over the Soviet Union. The city has shopping centres, a cultural centre, a seafront park, and promenade, a stadium, and nice sandy beaches. The industry in the north-west part of the town is separated from the housing districts along the seashore.

We now pass the pumps of the Baku water-supply system built 70 years ago.

Near the **town of Kilyazi** (about 50 miles from Baku) there is a turning to the **health resorts of Alty-agach** and **Gala-alty** ("under the rock"). Under the rocks here are thermal mineral springs of the Carpathian "Naphthusi"-type, good for treating the gallbladder disease and other ailments. There is a sanatorium for patients suffering from these illnesses. On top of a rocky hill nearby are the ruins of the Chirakh-kala fortress (17th century).

As this point we leave Greater Baku. On the left you can see the spurs of the Great Caucasus Range, the narrow coastal strip of the Samur-Divichi Plain on the right is cut across by nearly 60 small shallow rivers. The land is also irrigated by a canal continuing the Samur river to the north.

Beyond Samur near Derbent is a famous pass through the Caucasus—known in the past as *Bab-ul-abzab*, or the "Great Caspian Gate". Fortresses and ramparts built in the 5th–7th centuries defended the pass from nomads' raids: starting from the Beshbarmag Mountain they stretched for miles and were 30 ft. thick in places.

Mt. Beshbarmag is 55 miles from Baku, on your left. The two pointed peaks on the top of this mountain resemble fingers, there used to be five—hence its name, meaning "five fingers".

Beyond the **town of Siazan** which grew up around oil fields discovered in 1940, is the village Ghil-ghil-chai. Here too are the remains—evenly spaced earth ramparts—of ancient defences.

According to legend they were built by Alexander the Great to protect beautiful Queen Nushabe of Barda. Alexander, it is said, having heard of the

11th Red Army Memorial put up in memory of the revolutionary soldiers from Russia who helped the people of Baku to establish Soviet power here in April 1920.

queen's beauty, came to visit her under the alias of an ambassador. The queen, though, saw through the pretence. She impressed Alexander with her wisdom as well as beauty. Some time later Alexander received a report that Nushabe had been captured by the Kipchak tribes. He promptly moved against the Kipchaks and routed them, liberating the queen. Then he had the ramparts built to defend the local peaceful population from the savage tribes. This legend is reflected in one of Nizami's poems.

Divichi ("camel-driver" in translation) is an old village on the former caravan route. Today it is a district centre known for carpet weaving. Nearby is the site of Shaberan—a major Azerbaijan city founded in the 5th century, which was razed to the ground in the early 18th century. The site is being excavated—a lot of coins have been found produced by the local mint, one of the biggest mints in the East.

Oil refinery.

Hachmas, the centre of a vegetable growing district, has a large cannery. Early vegetables are supplied not only to Baku, but to Moscow, Leningrad and other cities. In the village of Shikhlar nearby is the 15th-century Sheikh Yussif Mosque.

KHOUDAT is the most ancient and northernmost of the capitals of Northern Azerbaijan principalities. The town is now a health resort. The small settlements of **Yalama** and **Nabran** in the vicinity are due to be turned into a major health and holiday zone on the scale of the Crimea or the Black Sea Caucasian coast. The fine natural and climatic conditions of the area—golden beaches, woods along the seashore, the backdrop of snow-capped mountains with rivers and waterfalls—make it an ideal spot for a holiday resort. Large funds have been allocated for the development of the area and in a few years' time it will be a major tourist attraction.

In summer you can visit the Yalama-Nabran holiday zone

One of the gardens in Kubá, known in Azerbaijan as "Orchard Town". Over 100 varieties of apples and pears are grown here.

and see where the ship-repair yard that you saw on your way to Kobustan has a holiday camp. The workers are holidaying here for free or at a large discount.

On the way back to Baku you can visit **KUBÁ**, one of the loveliest spots in the region: a city of gardens on the northeast slope of the Great Caucasus at a height of 2,000 ft. above sea level, on the Gudial-chai river. The centre of the principality was moved from Khudat to Kubá in the 18th century and the city grew in importance. The writer and educator Abaskhuli Bakikhanov spent his early years here, and his house is still preserved. Among the architectural sights are the 16th-century fortress, the 19th-century **Sakina-hanum** and **Djuma mosques**, the 19th-century **bathhouse** with two egg-shaped domes. Not far away in the mountains there is a **village**, called **Khanalyk**, which has a unique language of its own, now subject of special linguistic study. The village also has a 9th-century **fire-worshippers' temple.**

Typical Azerbaijan village scene.

Kubá is a fruit-growing centre: over a hundred varieties of apples and pears, dozens of varieties of plums, apricots, peaches, cherries, quince are cultivated. Adam Olearius, a 17th-century Austrian traveller who stayed some time here, mentions a local custom according to which every boy and girl were supposed to graft a hundred wild fruit trees and were not supposed to get married before the trees bore fruit—a custom that must have undoubtedly contributed to the local horticulture. Visits to the fruit farms as well as to the local carpet-factory—Kubá is equally famous for its carpets—can be arranged. One of the carpets, produced here—the 1712 *Gollu-Chichi* is exhibited in the New York Metropolitan Museum.

You can visit the famous Tengin Canyon that was admired by Dumas-père. If you go in for big game hunting licences for shooting the Caucasian goat, wild boar, or brown bear, can be obtained through the local Intourist branch in Baku.

Copper-smith at work.

SHEMAKHA—SHEKI—ZAKATALY

This last tour will take you across Azerbaijan to its northwest border and on to Georgia. It takes two or three days (depending on how long you stay in Sheki). The scenic route runs along the southern slopes of the Great Caucasus.

Having passed the township of Hydralan your bus takes the left turn to Shemakha. For a few dozen miles you ride through outlying parts of Kobustan—you will recognize its landscape: the dry steppe, rolling hills cut by ravines. The road keeps climbing and turning.

In the past there may have been dense forest here later destroyed by the activities of man, burnt down by the fires of the hordes of Kipchaks, Khazars, Mongols which rolled over the area; many a battle was fought as is witnessed by some of the local names: *Adjidere*—"bitter gorge", *Djanghi*—warriors' dance.

The **Diri-Baba Mausoleum**—near Maraza—was built in 1402 over a natural cave which formed the mausoleum's lower floor. An inscription tells us the name of the father of the man who built the mausoleum—"the son of Ustad Hadji..." The name of the builder himself, though, has been lost. The tomb was considered a holy place and is an interesting example of medieval architecture, its original design blending with the landscape.

The city of **SHEMAKHA** (80 miles from Baku) lies on a slope 2,600 ft. above sea level. One of the most ancient Oriental trading cities, it was mentioned by the Greek astronomer and geographer Claudius Ptolemy (2nd century A.D.) but the exact date of its foundation has not been established. Its name may be derived from *shah*—great and *makh*—city, though there are other explanations for it. Since the 6th century it has been the capital of Shirvan. Advantageously situated at the juncture of caravan routes linking Asia with Europe Shemakha was an important political, trade and cultural centre. Its magnificent bazaars saw a lively trade in silk, carpets, gold cloth, wool, arms. In the 16th century the English had trading stations here. About 50 well-known poets added "Shirvani" to their names—including Hagani, Nasimi, Sabir, Seid Azim, Abbas Sihat.

Few Azerbaijan cities have had such a splendid or tragic past. It was repeatedly sacked by Arab, Persian, Mongol, Turkish conquerors, razed to the ground by disastrous earthquakes. In the early 18th century the Persian Nadir-Shah, having destroyed Shemakha, resettled its population in "New Shemakha" (today only the ruins are left). But the old city was rebuilt. Unity with Russia in 1805 made Shemakha secure against raids, but the earthquakes of 1859, and particularly of 1902, again destroyed the city to the ground. Consequently, today Shemakha has an overall modern appearance, though some historical monuments have remained.

The *Eddi Giumbez* **(Seven cupolas) Shirvan Khans' Tomb** (18th–19th centuries) is in one of the city's many

Sheki Khans' Palace.

View of the interior of the palace.

cemeteries. The half-ruined cupolas and crooked tomb stones bear witness to the formidable earthquakes they had to withstand. The cemetery is on a hill commanding a good view of the city. The ruins of the **Gulistan Fortress** (10th–12th centuries) can be seen uphill.

Other places of interest include the 10th-century **Djuma Mosque**, restored after the 19th-century earthquake and now being restored again; the *ovdan* (15th century), the **house-museum of the poet Sabir**. Each May lovers of poetry from Baku and other places in Azerbaijan, from the other Union republics and Moscow come here to hold the traditional Days of Poetry.

This is one of the major grape-growing areas in Azerbaijan and the whole of the USSR. The land has been further improved and irrigated by the building of water reservoirs and other facilities in the 1970–80s. *Matrassa* is the name of Shemakha's unique grape variety and of the famous dry red wine made from it, winner of many international med-

als. You can visit the vineyards and taste the local wines. One of the villages near Shemakha is called **Saghian**—"cup-bearer".

You can visit the **Pirkuli Astrophysical Observatory**, 8 miles out of the city, 4,600 ft. above sea level. There are permanent groups of Bulgarian and the GDR scientists on the staff.

Shemakha with its mineral springs and fresh mountain air is a popular holiday spot and health resort. In summer it provides relief from the heat of Apsheron, in winter it is a good place for skiing and tobogganing. There is a tourist camp near the Pirkuli Observatory.

Intourist has a special one-day tour to Shemakha.

Having left Shemakha your bus keeps climbing the zigzag road to reach the **Akhsu Pass** at a height of nearly 3,200 ft. Make a short stop here and enjoy the splendid view of the mountains and Shirvan Valley, forming part of the Kura-Araks Plain.

You can see the ruins of "New Shemakha" not far from the small town of Akhsu with its tall poplars. There are some tombs, several of them dating to the 15th century, and a 16th-century bridge.

You descend from the pass in to **Shirvan Valley**, a cotton-growing area. In September you can witness the cotton-harvesting, largely mechanized, though there is still some hand-picking. The cotton crop has grown fourfold since the early 1970s.

You cross a few mountain rivers, small and unimpressive for most part of the year. Yet the big bridges which span them, the width of the pebbly river-beds and the watermarks left on the hill's sides—tell us that at high-flood time they are transformed into powerful torrents carrying away rocks and uprooted trees.

One of the biggest and calmest rivers—the **Geok-chai** (blue river) has given its name to the town and surrounding district known for its special pomegranates. Local industry includes a cannery making fruit juices and **narsharab**—a pomegranate sauce for meat and fish—indispensable in the Azerbaijan cuisine. The town's old plane-trees add to its charm. Drop in to the Plane-Tree tea-house and relax over a glass of Azerbaijan tea.

You now pass through the cotton-growing Agdash district. Most of the **Turianchai Nature Reserve** with its unique grove of prehistoric drought-resistant Eldar pines is situated in the region.

You turn north. Plains give way to hills as we again approach the Great Caucasus Range—the mountains loom larger and larger, in the distance you can distinguish the snow-capped summits. On the right is **Mount Bazardüzü** (14,800 ft.). The local explanation for this name goes as follows. The mountain is the focal point *(düzü)* of the bazaar of other mountain peaks round it.

We pass the **Haldan township**. The model secondary school here trains schoolchildren in agricultural skills: to drive tractors and harvesters, milk cows, plant crops, etc. The school has a commercial nursery and runs a poultry

Akhsu Pass (3,200 ft. above sea-level).

farm—all at a profit, which enables it to acquire new equipment, for instance, a close-circuit TV studio.

We now enter the Sheki district. The Ordjonikidze state-farm, the biggest grain-growing farm in the Caucasus, is situated on the fertile plain here.

The city of **SHEKI** (133 miles from Shemakha) is one of the oldest and biggest cities in Azerbaijan. There are reasons to suppose that it is 2,500 years old. In the 1st century B.C. the Saki tribe (after which the city is called) together with the Albanians beat Pompey's army. The town was subject, though, to frequent conquest and sacking. In the first half of the 18th century a local feudal lord, Hadji Chelebi, founded the Sheki Khanate which for a time was the most powerful in Azerbaijan. The Persian Nadir-Shah besieged the Sheki fortress without success.

There is a story connecting the name of a local fortress, Galasan-geresen (Come and see) with the answer given, it is said, by Hadji Chelebi to Nadir-Shah who asked what made the people of Sheki so bold as to refuse to submit to the Shah...

Sheki, like Shemakha, is situated on a mountain slope, over 2,200 ft. above sea level. It suffered badly from floods—the 1772 flood completely destroying the city. The rivers, which, as we have said, turn into avalanches during the rainy season, are even more formidable here than in Shirvan. The people of Sheki built themselves a new city near the village of Nukha. For two centuries it was known as Nukha. In 1960, however, it was decided to rename it Sheki.

The upper, ancient part of the city, has been turned into a historical museum. You will stay at one of the 18th-century caravanserais, still serving as a hotel. In the 18th-century fortress, you will see the summer palace of the Sheki Khans, interesting from the point of view of its architecture, wall paintings and decorative details. The stained-glass windows and wooden latticework provide original lighting. Most impressive of all are the wall paintings. On the first floor are frescoes of battles, hunting, every-day scenes, etc.

Other places to visit in Sheki are the **Mirza Fatali**

Akhundov Museum and the **Museum of the Revolution and Military Valour**, from which one gets an excellent view of the city; **Markhal recreation** zone with a hotel for the silk-mill workers; and the Seven Beauties restaurant serving national dishes.

Sheki, which comes fifth among the republic's cities in terms of its population (50,000), is a silk manufacturing centre. The Lenin Silk Mill employing 6,000 produces a wide range of silk textiles that have won a number of international prizes. There is also a factory producing clothes, a tobacco fermenting plant and other industries. Sheki is the centre of a major grain-producing and cattle-breeding area; it is also known for its high-grade tobacco and nuts (hazel and walnuts) accounting for a large proportion of the total USSR nut production. You can visit buffalo-breeding (the first in the USSR to introduce electric milking for buffaloes) and trout-breeding farms; as well as the gardens of an agro-industrial complex uniting ten collective farms.

Sheki is known for its handicrafts: painted chests, sheepskin hats, sugar candies coloured with various natural substances, *pahlava* pastry made of rice flour and nuts, *nabat*, and *peshmesh*, etc. An excellent Sheki souvenir is a woman's silk shawl.

Near the town of Kakhi you will see the grave of *Hadji Murat*, a follower of Shamil, leader of the resistance put up by the Caucasian mountain people to Russian colonization and to the feudal lords. This was the scene of the events described in Tolstoy's story *Hadji Murat.* Tolstoy visited these parts. The anthropologist and sculptor M. Gerassimov who worked out a method of recreating human features from sculls did a portrait of Hadji Murat. There is a 4th-century temple in the village of Kum and an 18th-century bridge and other buildings in the village of Ilissu.

The next 60 miles, stretching up to the border with Georgia, planted on both sides with nut-trees to protect it from land slips, is known as the **Nut Road**. It was built in the 19th century.

ZAKATALY (75 miles from Sheki) is a lovely green town

planted with plane-trees. In the centre there is a **Great Patriotic War Memorial** with an eternal flame. Wide stone steps lead up to the monument. Not far from it are the ruins of Shamil's stronghold (1830). Zakataly has a big nut-processing factory. There are rose nurseries in the district and rose oil and scent is made here.

North of the town is a forest reserve: oak, beach and hornbeam woods and mountain pastures. It is the habitat of the Caucasian goat, deer, chamois, roe, Caucasian mountain turkey, and other rare birds and animals.

Belokany is the last place we pass on our tour—the only area in the Caucasus where persimmons are grown.

Here we say good-bye, and you pass on to Georgia, to Telavi tourist centre (60 miles from Zakataly). The Azerbaijan word for good-bye is *sag öl* which also means "good health". We wish you all the best and hope to see you again!

Practical Information

FOREIGN TOURISM ORGANISATIONS

Azerbaijan Intourist Agency—65 Prospekt Neftyanikov, 92-87-13

Baku Intourist Agency—1 Prospekt Lenina, 98-93-93
Sputnik Youth Tourism Bureau—251 Pervomaiskaya Ulitsa, 93-18-43

HOTELS

Baku Intourist offers three categories of hotel accommodation (according to class of tour): luxe—a three-, two- or one-room suite with bathroom; first-class—a one- or two-bedded room with bathroom; tourist class—a one- or two-bedded room with wash basin. Children from 2 to 12 are charged halfprice, an additional bed can be installed in the parents' room.

Azerbaijan—1 Prospekt Lenina

600 double rooms, 46 luxe suites; three dining-rooms (band and disco in marble room), conference-hall, banqueting-hall, cafe, bar (foreign currency accepted), service bureau, tourist bureau, bank, foreign currency Chinar souvenir and book shop, delicatessen, post-office and telegraph, chemist's, clothes and footwear repairs, photo studio.

Intourist—63 Prospekt Neftyanikov

77 suites and rooms: 15 of them luxe and semi-luxe; 33—first class, the rest—tourist class; restaurant (band), banqueting-hall, cafe (disco), bar (foreign currency accepted), service bureau, post-office and telegraph, first aid post.

Moskva—1a Ulitsa Mekhti Huseinzade

99 luxe and semi-luxe suites: 11 of them three-room, 88—two-room; conference-hall seating 250, restaurant, two banqueting-halls, cafe (disco), service bureau, sauna, swimming pool.

International Ganjlik Youth Camp—Posyolok Zagoolba

RESTAURANTS

Azerbaijan cuisine appeals to all tastes. While having much in common with the cooking of the other Caucasian nationalities and Iran, Azerbaijan food has a character all of its own and is surprisingly varied—each region, as a rule, having its own specialities. As is the case with Azerbaijan carpets or music, the dishes are exquisitely refined and take time and skill to make. There are about a hundred varieties of pilaff: instead of being cooked in oil in one pot as in Uzbekistan, the rice and various seasonings (meat, fish, fruit, etc.) of the Azerbaijan pilaff are cooked in separate pots. At home they are served separately, with melted butter in a jug, and every one helps himself according to taste. In a restaurant the helpings are usually prepared and served in a metal dish with a lid. We also recommend the following dishes: *piti* soup, made of mutton and peas, served in an earthenware pot; *dovga* yoghurt soup served with meat balls and herbs; *kiufta-bosbash* soup served with large meat balls; the famous *liula-kebab* grilled over an open fire; *dooshbere* soup served with local kind of ravioli; *kutabi* pastries with various stuffings; and the Azerbaijan sweets—*sheker-bura, sheker-lockum, pahlava* accompanied by *sherbet* or tea. Tea, served in small glasses (*armuds*), starts off and ends a meal. Black tea (the Azerbaijanis do not drink green tea) replaces wine in everyday meals, wine only being drunk on special occasions.

Apart from the restaurants mentioned in our tours, the following serve national Azerbaijan dishes:

Gulistan—1 Kommunisticheskaya Ulitsa

Banqueting-hall, national cuisine dining-room, tea-room, 5 bars, "mother and child" cafe, cinema, souvenir shop, variety show. Wide choice of national dishes, sweets, drinks. House specialities. Open: 7 p.m. to midnight.

Azerbaijan—1 Prospekt Lenina.

Three dining-rooms: the Carpet Room, the Mirror Room, and the Marble Room. Eastern and European cuisine, two bands and disco, bar (foreign currency accepted). Open: noon to midnight.

Intourist—63 Prospekt Neftyanikov

A main dining-room and a banqueting-hall, bar, Eastern and European cuisine, band. Open: 8 p.m. to midnight.

Moscow—1a Ulitsa Mekhti Husseinzade

A main dining-room and two banqueting-halls, cafe, bar, national and European cuisine, Azerbaijan wines and brandies, band, open-air patio in summer. Open: 8 p.m. to midnight.

Baky—13 Voroshilovskaya Ulitsa

Two dining-rooms, a banqueting-hall, bar, national cuisine, band. Open: noon to midnight.

SHOPS

Department stores are open (seven days a week, no lunch break) from 9 a.m. to 8 p.m. Food stores are also open seven days a week. Other shops, as a rule, are open week days from 10 a.m. to 7 p.m. (Lunch break 2 to 3 p.m.) Closed Sundays.

Baku offers a wide choice of souvenirs made of ceramics, wood, metal; jewellery made of common and precious metals. A good memento is a rug or printed shawl, or an embroidered velvet cushion case. Embroidered shoes *charykhs* make comfortable slippers; in miniature form, they can be hung on the wall as decoration, or used as pin-cushions. The following also make attractive presents: records of *mugam* folk music; sets of *armud* tea glasses; Azerbaijan tea, wines (Matrassa, Sadymly, Martuni, Shemakha) and brandies (Moscow, Gei-Gyol, Shirvan, Jubilee, Azerbaijan). Apart from the souvenir stall in your hotel, you can buy souvenirs at:

Baky Department Store—33/35 Ulitsa Hadjibeckova
Central Department Store—5 Ulitsa Ali Bairamova
Bakinski Department Store—3 Ulitsa Shaumiana
Podarki (Gifts) shops—60 Ulitsa Nizami, 4 Ulitsa Dvadtsat Vosmogo Aprelya
Souveniry shop—8 Ulitsa Kolomeitseva
Chinar shop—103 Prospekt Neftyanikov
Art Salon—60 Ulitsa Nizami
Iskousstvo (Art) (books on art, albums)—29 Ulitsa Saratovtsa-Yefimova
Almaz (Diamond) jewellery shop—4 Ulitsa Mushfiga
Izumrud (Emerald) jewellery shop—68 Ulitsa Nizami
Firiousa (Turquoise) jewellery shop—11 Ulitsa Zevina
Second-hand jewellery shop—7 Ulitsa Zevina
Dom Knigi (House of Books)—2 Ulitsa Voroshilova
Dom gramplastinok (House of Records)—528 Prospekt Narimanova
Melodiya shop (records)—11 Ulitsa Zevina
Tarané (music shop)—23 Ulitsa Hadjieva
Perfumery—60 Ulitsa Nizami

MARKETS

Central—7 a.m. to 8 p.m.—63 Ulitsa Vurguna
Sharg Bazary—8 a.m. to 7 p.m.—11/5 Moskovskiy Prospekt
Passage—7 a.m. to 7 p.m.—12/14 Ulitsa Saratovtsa-Yefimova
Armenikendskiy—8 a.m. to 8 p.m.—100 Prospekt Lenina

POST, TELEGRAPH, TELEPHONE

Central Telegraph Office—41 Ulitsa Shaumiana
Central Post Office—41 Ulitsa Shaumiana
Long-distance telephone call bookings—07
Urgent telephone calls are charged at treble rate

TRANSPORT

The trolley-buses, buses and underground (metro) run from 6 a.m. to 1 a.m. The trams—from 5 a.m. to 2 a.m.
Fares: 3 kopecks—tram, 4 kopecks—trolley-bus, 5 kopecks—bus and underground, irrespective of distance on one route; no conductor service, small change or tickets (separate for each form of transport) should be prepared in advance. Books of tickets can be obtained at stops or from news-stalls.
Taxis—24-hour service. Taxis can be distinguished by their checker board pattern; a green light on the windscreen or roof top indicates that the vehicle is free. The basic charge is 20 kopecks per km., plus a 20-kopeck hire charge; one hour wait costs 2 roubles.

THEATRES, CONCERT HALLS

Plays start at 7.30 p.m.; concerts—at 8 p.m.; they end at about 11 p.m. No performances Mondays.
Cloakroom free of charge; cost of renting binoculars—30–50 kopecks.
Akhundov Opera and Ballet Theatre—8 Ulitsa Dvadtsat Vosmogo Aprelya
Azizbeckov Drama Theatre—Ploshchad Fizuli
Kurbanov Musical Comedy Theatre—8 Ulitsa Shaumiana
Vurgun Russian Drama Theatre—7 Ulitsa Hagani
Azerbaijan State Theatre of Song—36 Prospekt Neftyanikov
Puppet Theatre—36 Prospekt Neftyanikov
Actors' Club—10 Ulitsa Hagani

Circus—68 Ulitsa Sameda Vurguna
Magomayev Philharmonic Society and Summer Concert and Variety Hall—2 Kommunisticheskaya Ulitsa
Concert Hall of the Lenin Palace of Culture—37 Prospekt Kirova
Hadjibeckov Conservatoire—98 Ulitsa Dimitrova

CINEMAS

First show 10 a.m., last show over before midnight. No admission after the beginning of a performance (except at the Billick cinema for documentaries and popular-science films). Programmes usually include a newsreel or documentary and a feature film; they last for about two hours. No cloakroom. No smoking. Seats numbered.

Nizami—20 Prospekt Kirova
Azerbaijan—9 Ulitsa Djaparidze
Veten—41 Ulitsa Karganova
Araz—3 Ulitsa Azizbeckova
Billick—104 Ulitsa Nizami

MUSEUMS, EXHIBITIONS

Azerbaijan History Museum—4 Ulitsa Malygina. Open: 11.30 a.m. to 5 p.m., except Friday.
House of Friendship of the Peoples of the USSR—1 Ulitsa Lermontova. Open: 9 a.m. to 6 p.m.
Baku Branch of the Central Lenin Museum—123 Prospekt Neftyanikov. Open: 11.30 a.m. to 7 p.m., except Monday.
Mustafayev Museum of Fine Arts—9 Ulitsa Chkalova. Open: 10.30 a.m. to 6 p.m., except Monday.
Museum of Carpets and Folk Crafts—*Ichery-Sheker* (Old City). Open: 10.30 a.m. to 6 p.m.
Shirvan-Shahs' Palace—76 Zamkovski Pereulok. Open: 10.30 a.m. to 6 p.m.
Nizami Literary Museum—33 Ulitsa Kommunisticheskaya. Open: noon to 5 p.m., except Saturday and Sunday.
Museum of 18th Army—9 Ulitsa Miasnikova. Open: 10.30 a.m. to 6 p.m., except Monday.
Museum of Education—11 Ulitsa Chkalova. Open: 9 a.m. to 5 p.m., except Sunday.
Djaffar Djabarly Theatre Museum—24 Ulitsa Karayeva. Open: 9 a.m. to 6 p.m., except Saturday and Sunday.

Museum of Atheism—9 Ulitsa Menzhinskogo. Open: 9 a.m. to 6 p.m., except Saturday and Sunday.
Museum of Azerbaijan Music—9 Ulitsa Menzhinskogo. Open: 9 a.m. to 6 p.m., except Saturday and Sunday.
Zardabi Museum of Natural History—3 Ulitsa Lermontova. Open: 9 a.m. to 5 p.m., except Saturday and Sunday.
Narimanov Memorial Museum—15/17 Kommunisticheskaya Ulitsa. Open: 10.30 a.m. to 6 p.m.
Hadjibeckov Museum—67 Ulitsa Ketskhoveli. Open: 9. a.m. to 6 p.m.
Azimzade Flat-Museum—157 Pervomaiskaya Ulitsa. Open: 9 a.m. to 6 p.m.
Mamadkulizade Museum—56 Ulitsa Ostrovskogo. Open: 9 a.m. to 6 p.m., except Saturday and Sunday.
Samed Vurgun Museum—4 Ulitsa Miasnikova. Open: 10.30. a.m. to 6 p.m., except Friday.
Djabarly Museum—44 Ulitsa Sultanova. Open: 9 a.m. to 6 p.m., except Saturday and Sunday.
Biul-Biul Flat-Museum—19 Ulitsa Hagani. Open: 9 a.m. to 6 p.m., except Saturday and Sunday.
Ordubady Flat-Museum—19 Ulitsa Hagani. Open: 9 a.m. to 6 p.m., except Saturday and Sunday.
Shaumian Flat-Museum—15 Ulitsa Hadjibeckova. Open: 10.30. a.m. to 6 p.m.
Azizbeckov Flat-Museum—105 Ulitsa Montina. Open: 10 a.m. to 7 p.m., except Monday.
Djaparidze Flat-Museum—corner of Ulitsa Nizami and Prospekt Lenina. Open: 10 a.m. to 7 p.m., except Monday.
Kirov Flat-Museum—18 Ulitsa Hagani. Open: 11 a.m. to 7 p.m., except Monday.
Memorial Museum of the Underground Printing-Press "Nina"—102 Ulitsa Iskrovskaya. Every day except Monday.
Exhibition of Economic Achievements—Primorskiy Boulevard. Open: 9 a.m. to 6 p.m.
Art Gallery—27 Ulitsa Hadjibeckova. Open: 11 a.m. to 5.30 p.m., except Monday.
Samedova Art Salon—19 Ulitsa Hagani. Open: 9 a.m. to 6 p.m., except Monday.

PARKS

Primorskiy Park (seafront park)—Prospekt Neftyanikov
Park Kirova—6 Ulitsa Lermontova
Park Dzerzhinskogo—35 Ulitsa Chapaeva

Park Druzhby (Friendship Park)—Shikhov
Zoopark (Zoo)—39 Ulitsa Bakihanova

SPORTS FACILITIES

Palace of Sports—12 Prospekt Kirova
Lenin Stadium—1 Tbilisskiy Prospekt
Spartak Stadium—Leningradskiy Prospekt
Racecourse—109 Prospekt Narimanova
Swimming pools—Prospekt Narimanova (covered), 6A, Ulitsa Dvadtsati Shesti Bakinskikh Komissarov (open)

USEFUL ADDRESSES AND TELEPHONES

Weather Forecast Bureau—3 Ulitsa Karganova, tel. 93-95-78 (automatic answering service), 93-80-36 (duty officer)
Time—tel. 06
Interpreter-Guides' Bureau—98-93-95
Photographic equipment shop—23/25 Ulitsa Druzhba Molodyozhi, tel. 62-56-61
Sound Recording Studio—9 Ulitsa Hadjibeckova, tel. 92-15-01; 27 Ulitsa Druzhba Molodyozhi, tel. 62-62-85.
"Sea Trip" Launch Pier—Every day 10.30 a.m. to 5 p.m. (Holiday period to 7 p.m.). Fares: 35 kopecks—adults, 10 kopecks—children
Ambulance—tel. 03
Police—tel. 02
Lost Property Office—39 Ulitsa Gogolya, tel. 98-21-19

INTOURIST ITINERARIES

One-day Programme

Morning—3-hour bus tour "Baku, the Capital of Azerbaijan". Starting-point: Government House, Ploshchad Lenina. Tour of main sights and monuments of architecture. Information provided on the history and present-day life of Baku and the republic as a whole.

Afternoon—tour of Apsheron, past the oldest oil-fields to the unique Ateshgah fire-worship temple. During your free time from 5 p.m. to 7 p.m. we suggest a walk to the Shirvan-Shahs' Palace and back following the route given in the 3rd Tour of our guidebook, or a visit to the Museum of Carpets and Folk Crafts.

Evening—dinner at the Bukhara restaurant in the Old City (national cuisine); a walk along the seafront boulevard, or a sea trip in a motor boat if you have the time.

Two-day Programme

1st Day. Morning—tour of the city and visit to the fire-worship temple Ateshgah. Afternoon free—we suggest a visit to the Azerbaijan Historical Museum and a walk round the district in which the museum is located (as per the end of the 1st Tour in our guide-book). Evening—dinner at the Bukhara restaurant.

2nd Day. Morning—tour of the Old City and the Shirvan-Shahs' Palace. Afternoon—tour of Apsheron including a visit to the Serebrovsky oil and gas sea-platforms. Evening—opera, concert, or circus visit, or—for those who prefer it—another walk round the town. We suggest you start at the Philharmonic Society building, walk down through Revolution Garden to Ploshchad Azneft, dropping in at the Hoshbaht tea-room on the way, then take a cable-car ride up to Nagorny Park (Mountain Park) to see the evening panorama of Baku, a ride back down, finishing up with a walk along the seafront.

Three-day Programme

The first two days as above.

3rd Day. Morning—trip to Kobustan. Afternoon free (have a look at the suggested walking tours in our guide-book). Evening—visit to one of the factories, organizations, etc., that are collective members of the Society of Friendship and Cultural Links with Foreign Countries.

For those with more time at their disposal we suggest the tours outside Baku, including the tour across Azerbaijan into Georgia.

The suggested itineraries can be altered or expanded. Depending on season and a tourist's professional interests visits to factories, research and educational institutions, artists' or writers' unions, clubs, artists' studios or research laboratories, etc., can be arranged.

All inquiries should be addressed to the Baku branch of Intourist or to your hotel service bureau.

REQUEST TO READERS

Raduga Publishers would be glad to have your opinion of this book, its translation and design and any suggestions you may have for future publications.
Please send all your comments to 17, Zubovsky Boulevard, Moscow, USSR.

ИБ № 1816
Редактор русского текста *М. Державина*
Контрольный редактор *И. Вишневская*
Художник *А. Попова*
Художественный редактор *А. Томчинская*
Технические редакторы *А. Агафошина, Н. Должикова*
Сдано в набор 19.06.86. Подписано в печать 24.04.87. Формат 84 × 108 ^{1}/$_{32}$. Бумага мелованная. Гарнитура универс. Печать офсетная. Условн. печ. л. 10,50. Усл. кр.-отт. 54,14. Уч.-изд. л. 11,55. Тираж 16 170 экз. Заказ № 005738. Цена 1 р. 60 к. Изд. № 1816. Издательство «Радуга» Государственного комитета СССР по делам издательств, полиграфии и книжной торговли.
Москва, 119859, Зубовский бульвар, 17.
Изготовлено в ГДР

1. Apsheron Hotel
2. Monument to V. I. Lenin
3. Azerbaijan Hotel
4. Dynamo Stadium
5. Dzerzhinsky Club
6. Dvadtsat Shest Bakinskikh Komissarov Metro Station
7. V. I. Lenin Museum
8. The Pearl Restaurant
9. Azerbaijan Historical Museum
10. Baky Department Store
11. Kurbanov Musical Comedy Theatre
12. Puppet Theatre
13. Maiden Tower (*Gyz Galassy*)
14. Shirvan-Shahs' Palace
15. Philharmonic Society
16. Mustafayev Museum of Fine Arts
17. Yuri Gagarin Palace of Young Pioneers
18. Open-air Cinema
19. Cable-railway Station
20. Intourist Hotel
21. Azerbaijan Intourist Agency
22. Monument to S. Kirov
23. House of Friendship of the Peoples of the USSR
24. Moskva Hotel
25. Baky Soveti Metro Station
26. Palace of Weddings
27. Monument to Nizami
28. Nizami Literary Museum
29. Central Department Store
30. Monument to Fizuli
31. Azizbeckov Drama Theatre
32. Tara-Pir Mosque
33. Nizami Metro Station
34. Samed Vurgun Russian Drama Theatre
35. Actors' Club
36. 26 Baku Commissars' Memorial
37. Sergei Kirov Flat-Museum
38. Akhundov State Public Library
39. Children's Theatre
40. Akhundov Opera and Ballet Theatre
41. Eastern Sweets Shop
42. Nizami Cinema
43. Hadjibeckov Conservatoire
44. Lenin Palace of Culture
45. Central Collective Farmers' Market
46. Memorial Museum of the Underground Printing-Press "Nina"
47. Circus
48. Sabunchinsky Railway Station
49. Dvadtsat Vosmogo Aprelya Metro Station
50. Railway Station
51. Karabakh Hotel
52. Lenin Stadium
53. Shaumian Metro Station
54. Shaumian Palace of Culture
55. Passenger Seaport